Slovak Mass Media in the 21st Century: Current Challenges

STUDIES IN COMMUNICATION AND POLITICS

Edited by Bogusława Dobek-Ostrowska and Michał Głowacki

VOL. 10

Notes on the quality assurance and peer review of this publication

Prior to publication, the quality of the work published in this series
is reviewed by an external referee appointed by the editorship.

Miroslava Dobrotková / Artur Bckmatov /
Andrea Chlebcová Hečková / Ján Kuciak

Slovak Mass Media in the
21st Century: Current Challenges

PETER LANG

Bibliographic Information published by the Deutsche Nationalbibliothek
The Deutsche Nationalbibliothek lists this publication in the Deutsche
Nationalbibliografie; detailed bibliographic data is available in the internet
at http://dnb.d-nb.de.

Library of Congress Cataloging-in-Publication Data
A CIP catalog record for this book has been applied for at the
Library of Congress.

ISSN 2197-1625
ISBN 978-3-631-79634-4 (Print) • E-ISBN 978-3-631-79999-4 (E-PDF) •
E-ISBN 978-3-631-80000-3 (EPUB) • E-ISBN 978-3-631-80001-0 (MOBI)
DOI 10.3726/b16059

© Peter Lang GmbH
Internationaler Verlag der Wissenschaften
Berlin 2019
All rights reserved.

Peter Lang – Berlin · Bern · Bruxelles · New York ·
Oxford · Warszawa · Wien

This publication has been peer reviewed.

www.peterlang.com

This monograph is dedicated to the memory of our colleague Ján Kuciak, the journalist, who devoted himself body and soul to his work and who humanely, courageously and honestly sought the truth. He believed that the truth is the right way to the better and fairer future.

His beliefs have become immortal to us.

Authors.

Contents

Introduction

The development of Slovak media environment in the last 25 years is determined by turbulent political situation, the transition from socialist state system to the building and consolidating of democracy. Before 1989, the crucial function of media includes support of actual political leading power in preserving the status quo, communist propaganda and spreading only the official information. Mainly in the first years after the Velvet Revolution, the work of some media had common features with socialist media, especially during the so-called Mečiar era. Dual broadcasting system in Slovakia was established only in 1991 (before 1989, there were only state broadcasters) when public service media were created; however, from the beginning of the public broadcast, experts were discussing which system would guarantee real independence of public service media from politics. Nowadays, Slovak media operate on free market; their freedom of expression and the right to be informed is anyhow protected. Slovak media are confronted with the mistrust of the public and criticism of different aspects of their work – from alleged unprofessionalism and spreading distorted information to the dissemination of the facts that are not important and on the other hand marginalizing the facts that are necessary for the everyday decision-making of public.

This monograph deals with the most significant issues that are matters of public criticism. It has no ambition to cover all the problems which Slovak Mass Media actually face, but it is focused on the most challenging questions which actually resonate with the Slovak society. These are especially the role of media in the context of power control, sense of existence and funding of media of public service, corruption, spreading stereotypes by media and plurality of information and alternative media. In this regard, the work follows the research of Cillingová et al. titled *Current Issues of Slovak Mass Media*, published in 2019.

This monograph is divided into four chapters. In the first chapter named *"Crisis of Mass Media and its Influence on Power Control in Slovakia,"* the author defines the current situation in Slovak journalism, including its negative side, and explains how the political changes after 1989 have influenced the development of Slovak media market. The chapter interestingly describes how the theme of corruption penetrated the public discussion and on the other side, how the most powerful politicians tried to cease the dissemination of inconvenient information. The second chapter named *"Current Issues of Presenting of Stereotypes in Mass Media"* examines the stereotypes spread by media (especially internet and social media) in the context of its integrating function. On the basis of analyzing concrete news related to the education of Roma children, the author explains how the personal attitude marked by prejudices can influence the final text of news and how the simplification of information and neglect of journalists' duties (as the duty to verify the information) lead to the dissemination of disinformation and in the end even to the confirmation of prejudices. The third chapter titled *"Current issues of Public Media"* tries to explain why the role of public service media is irreplaceable. In the current social atmosphere, when the funding of public service media is considered as irresponsible spending of public and state finance, it describes that in relation to public service media the relevant question does not sound what fiscal profit such media could produce, but how public service media could contribute to public discussion and awareness. The issue of the last chapter is *"Phenomenon of Alternative Media in Slovakia."* First at all, the author defines which type of media shall be possibly identified as alternative and maps a short (for this moment) history of such media. Although the author points out the situations in which the alternative media fail to inform truthfully, impartially and objectively, on the other hand, he also questions the critics of alternative news when he remains that this criticism often does not take into account the difference between propaganda and relevant politic PR.

We believe that this monograph will be a valuable contribution to the academic and public discussion about the current situation in Slovak media system and about the future measures that are needed to be implemented with the aim to raise the awareness of Slovak public.

1 Crisis of Mass Media and Its Influence on Power Control in Slovakia

> *"Political actions and opinions of informed citizens are their own ones. Political actions and opinions of those who are partly informed pertain to those who partly informed them."[1]*

The thought of James Russell Wiggins, the chief director of the American daily Washington Post from the first half of the 20th century, relatively accurately expresses how important role, while forming and executing political power in a democratic country, communication channels play that is used for spreading information. Until recently, this privilege belonged to media, especially print, radio and television. Nowadays, the Internet has become an inseparable part of standard information channels. It is used by media houses, originally associated with the mentioned communication channels, by new media focused on publishing online as well as individuals, political, advertising or other groupings. Responsibility for spreading complex and verified information, however, in the eyes of the public and a majority of academic scholars falls under the responsibility of media and their publishers. New trends connected to unprecedented approach to communication channels for the general public brought them unknown competition as well as specific economic problems (to a substantial extent connected to financial and economic crisis rooted in 2008 and 2009).

Problems that affected the largest and most diversified systems in the Western world have to be dealt with by media in Slovakia too. Moreover, media system in the country went through relatively specific development with historically different experiences and influences compared to the typical media systems in the United States, Great Britain or Germany

---

1 Mintz, "Why is investigative journalism underrated and overrated at the same time".120.

that are considered to be models of high-quality, objective, deep and fair journalism. The social-political context where Slovak media developed was also different – from the time period of the acknowledgment of Slovak identity in Hungary and Austria-Hungary through the short era of democracy during the first Czechoslovak Republic and following the period of the clerofascist Slovak state to ten years of communism and subsequent establishment of democracy after 1989. Political-social conditions especially have influence on the formation and character of media in the national system. Political power in the country regulates legislative frameworks for a journalist, it provides them with tools for gaining information and respectively it limits their availability. On the other hand, society determines the importance of information published by the media, what steps will be taken concerning them and in what way it will force the responsibility towards those who were delegated by the power to administer the state.

In the entire spectrum of communication channels, primarily media still bring important information that nobody is interested in its initial spreading. Specific position belongs to discourses representing the role of media to control public and political power in the country with investigative types of communication as their more specific category. There is unwillingness of power to be controlled and its interest in hiding information potentially demonstrating malpractice of administration of public affairs and at the same time the expected interest of the public not to repeat the described situations by the investigative journalists. If power control works and investigative journalism brings high-quality, reliable and precisely elaborated information on malpractice of representatives of the state power, the public should be able and willing to ask their elected representatives for careful remedy of their malpractice and take responsibility against people and institutions that committed them.

The country where all the elements of the mentioned chain would work at 100% may not be found anywhere in the world although there are significant differences between individual national state-administrative systems and their institutions at first sight. For instance, Hungarian academic scholars observed how the same two cases may have different outcome based on the country of their occurrence. *"While the scandal involving British MPs led to substantial political and legal consequences, the similar scandal of Hungarian MPs at the same time practically caused neither legal nor political consequences.*"[2]

If we have a look at the functioning of media as a watchdog of democracy, while taking this contribution into consideration, it is relatively simple to identify national media systems where media pressure may bring results in the form of system remedy as well as those where media pressure brings results only occasionally or it does not exist at all and critical media are suppressed or completely destroyed by the power. There have been many levels of changes regarding Slovak media system; however, its media still did not reach the level of their most reputable foreign models of the highest quality. Many academic scholars agree to the fact that nowadays there are media of the highest quality we have ever had. A writer and journalist Karel Hvížďala[3] or former chief director of International Press Institute in Slovakia Pavol Múdry refers to this fact[4]. Both presented their opinion in interviews which content was especially focused on criticism of current media and journalists, respectively and their worries about their future. It also may suggest that historical comparison in such a young media system as the Slovak (Czech) may not succeed, and the actual work of media is supposed to meet much stricter criteria than comparison with its limited forerunners.

Therefore, at present, journalism in Slovakia faces very important challenges in the field of power control. On one hand, it has relative freedom (freedom of speech is on a high level), many tools for gaining information, first-experienced generation of journalists who started their careers after 1989 and free access to communication canals. On the other hand, it does not have enough financial resources and material security; it faces concentration of ownership in the hands of local financial groups, leaving of traditional media investors and decreasing trust in relation to the public; there are missing platforms for national or even international collaboration of journalists; it is limited to the extent of national market;

---

2   Bajomi-Lázár and Lampé, "Invisible journalism? The political impact of investigative journalism in Hungary", 33.

3   Struhárik, „Spisovateľ a novinár Karel Hvížďala: Naše médiá ešte nikdy neboli lepšie", online.

4   Mrvová, „Exšéf IPI: Naši novinári si kontrolu moci pomýlili s bezbrehou kritikou", online.

and it lacks the support of critical part of the public when informing on slips of the power and pressure on taking responsibility.

Besides the aforementioned, Slovak journalism is supposed to accept the fact that it does not exist in an isolated space, and in the globalized world, it is more and more dependent on connections exceeding state borders. It is the case of investigative journalists who nowadays, however, sporadically bring information gained, thanks to collaboration with their foreign colleagues (e.g., Panama Papers[5]).

All the mentioned circumstances and influences contribute to the current state of Slovak journalism and also to its part that is responsible for inspecting the activity of people who hold the power delegated by the public. In modern history, the Slovak media system met with apathy in times of Mečiar's government, commitment accompanied by the fall of Vladimír Mečiar and commencement of Mikuláš Dzurinda until (alleged) hypercriticism often interpreted by the public as simplification that all politicians are equally bad. Alternative media, propaganda channels and other activities with hardly identifiable authors and goals occurred. The public could not observe such a complex media system and independently assessed credibility and relevance of individual discourses. The task of media is, therefore, to mediate the public information truly and trustfully around the world itself, what is nowadays maybe more important than it was in the past.

1.1 Corruption and Politics in Slovakia after 1989

As mentioned in the previous text, social-political environment and its specification play a significant role in the creating and forming of media system in the country. To make media able to control the performance of delegated power, they need to have adequate conditions, and at the same time, there needs to be public interest in controlling the power. A Czech academic scholar Václav Štětka referring to Diamond, Przeworský, Stokes, Manin, Morlin and Schmitter writes that "the ability of population to enforce the responsibility of the government, elected representatives and other representatives of the state power is widely considered to be one

---

5 ČTK, pol, „Vznikol slovenský tím pre Panama Papers. Kauza spojila novinárov", online.

of the fundamental components and building stone of democracy."[6] According to Štětka, the corruption impoverishes the society because it decreases economic growth, demotivates businessmen and robs the state. "Corruption also subverts liberal democracy because political elites violate legal boundaries of their power, residents lose their trust in state institutions and civil society is suppressed by limited by power networks."[7]

After the Velvet Revolution, Slovakia went on a journey of democracy and later independence. Although the political development was more complicated, for purposes of this work, it is sufficient to designate the first years as the period of so-called mečiarizmus- governments of the Prime Minister Vladmír Mečiar until 1998. The first years after the Revolution necessarily had signs of the former regime and were marked by transformation in all fields. Authors such as Sičáková-Beblavá, Šípoš and Kurian while interpreting the transformation in the field of corruption are based on the ideas of Bulgarian intellectual Ivan Krastev. He pointed out at the fact that "corruption and privileges were one of the main features of *real socialism*" whereas privileges were for nomenclature and corruption for people. Nothing was legal but everything was possible.[8] Krastev concludes that people do not perceive various forms of corruption in the same way. They were used to the system of connection while gaining advantages and their position in the society. *"Transformation, however, brought the change and the need for connection was to the certain extent replaced with briberies."*[9] Štětka referring to Holmes regarding heritage after communism adds *"blurry boundaries between state institutions with each other and between the state and society."*[10]

Based on the analysis of Sičáková-Beblavá, Šípoš and Kurian, it was shown that corruption was not a strong political topic in the first years after revolution. The number of identified and solved cases of corruption

---

6 Štětka, "The watchdogs that only bark? Media and political Accountability in Central and Eastern Europe", 1.
7 Ibid., 3.
8 Sičáková-Beblavá, Šípoš and Kurian, „Korupcia a protikorupčná politika na Slovensku 1989 – 2010", 160.
9 Ibid., 160.
10 Štětka, "The watchdogs that only bark? Media and political Accountability in Central and Eastern Europe", 3.

was in the individual years until 1999, not even one-fifth compared to the following years.[11] In policy statements of six governments from revolution until 1998, the word "corruption" appeared only twice in total (for comparison, in the policy statement after the declaration of the first government of M. Dzurinda it was 12 times).[12] Based on proposed and enforced measures and commitments, the authors concluded that until 1998 the corruption was either a weak or no political topic at all. In the following period, it was a strong or moderately strong topic.[13] The most powerful topic connected to corruption was privatization of state property and state enterprises, back then required by transition to market economy. Estimates on the number and extent of corruption cases connected to the government of Vladimír Mečiar vary; however, many affairs still remain an example of improper administration of the government power and absolutely insufficient monitoring by media and society. They were not only economic affairs such as Nafta Gbely, Drukos, state banks but often political such as kidnapping of the president's son Michal Kováč junior or the murder of Róbert Remiáš and many others. Some of them connected to media will be closely elaborated in the following chapter.

In 1998, the direction of Slovakia in the field of fighting against corruption and the possibility to control the public power changed in the elections that are considered to be the most important in the history of independence. The government was constituted by Mikulár Dzurinda for the first time ending the era of mečiarizmus, and the space for important reforms was opened. *"Priority in the strategy of the fight against corruption was removal of its social causes especially the renewal of activity of market mechanism and regarding legal field it was renewal of punishability of active bribery and implementation of international conventions in the field of fight against corruption,"* as Ivan Mikloš, its former vice-chairman, summarized the goals of a new government in 2001.[14] Mikloš defined corruption as "misuse of power over foreign property or rights to gain own private advantages."

---

11 Sičáková-Beblavá, Šípoš and Kurian, „Korupcia a protikorupčná politika na Slovensku 1989–2010", 159.
12 Ibid., 168.
13 Ibid., 172.
14 Mikloš, „Správa o boji proti korupcii na Slovensku", 10.

"It is one of the most topical issues nowadays we have to deal with."[15] At the same time, Mikloš established eight crucial measures of the government to fight against corruption: establishment of National Anti-Corruption Unit at General Prosecution (2000), establishment of Bureau of the Fight against Corruption of the Office of Organized Crime (1998), establishment of Special Anti-corruption Unit within the Office of Prosecutor General, establishment of the Office for Public Procurement (2001), Supreme Audit Office (2001), National Security Authority (2001), adopting of Act on Free Access to Information (2000), and establishment of Business Register on the Internet (2001).[16] Almost all of the mentioned institutes are active nowadays, or they are modified and divided into the separate units, respectively.

Expectations of analysts, journalists or publicists, however, for first government of M. Dzurinda did not fully meet. *"Methods of Dzurinda's government and state bureaucrats administering the country since the times of Vladimír Mečiar in 1994–98 did not dramatically change as it was promised to the public. In the process of privatization, in management of state enterprises, at courts and in the system of health care are present people who are equally willing to undergo investigation as their forerunners,"* as it was written by an investigative journalist of Canadian origin Tom Nicholson.[17] Analysts who observed one of the most sensitive points of anti-corruption fight – privatization – reacted in a similar way. *"Promises to increase transparency in state enterprises, to disclose information about spending huge resources from funds for foreign help, to disclose information about privatization still remain in a written form only."*[18] Gorilla scandal proved the statements of Nicholson and analysts Zemanová and Sičáková to be true ten years later – disclosure of a document describing corruption at privatization of state enterprises during the Mikuláš Dzurinda's government in 2005–2006. Document was allegedly the transcription of dialogs in a conspiracy flat where representatives of Penta financial group with several politicians agreed on commissions from the selling of state

---

15 Ibid., 10.
16 Ibid., 12.
17 Nicholson, „Investigatívna žurnalistika na Slovensku: nátlak na zneváženie etiky", 103.
18 Zemanovičová and Sičáková, „Hovoriť o korupcii je málo", 8.

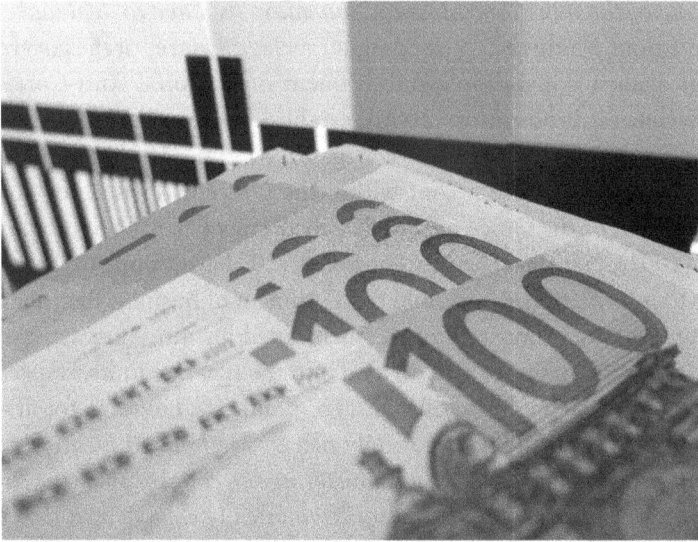

Image 1: Corruption and media (Author of photo: Lenka Banášová, private archive)

property. Wiretapping of the flat was carried out by the Slovak Information Service, but it was still not proved if the transcription disclosed anonymously on the Internet corresponds with the content of audio recordings from wiretapping.

Critical view on adopting of anti-corruption measure was presented by Vladimír Pirošík as well. His criticism referred to charging of the access to information because the act allowed office workers to decide how much money they charge for information. Charging became the tool for restricting the access to information. *"Regarding the costs for accessible information, strict and non-controversial § 21 of the Act on Free Access to Information containing the amendment of the particular institute is successfully accompanied by dilettantism of the ministry of finance in connection to office fantasies of individual obligatory persons."*[19]

---

19 Pirošík, „Zákon o slobodnom prístupe k informáciám: štruktúra a uplatňovanie", 60.

Vice versa, various observers also noticed indisputable positives brought by the government change. For instance, a media analyst Andrej Školkay emphasized the improvement of political culture and more sensitive reactions of elected representatives on criticism of the public and media since *"recently several ministers resigned in Slovakia due to various affairs presented in media whereas more serious affairs changed nothing before."*[20] In a similar positive way, some measures of the government of Mikuláš Dzurinda were also assessed by the analysts of Transparency International Slovakia who had no doubts about the fact that especially these governments mostly contributed to the fight against corruption and availability of information for public and media, too. The most successful fields are considered to be the activity of business register, land register and improvement of bank sector. *"Economic tools aimed at balancing demand and supply for their services and strengthening of capacities of these particular institutions helped all of these three fields on their way to remove corruption."*[21] Sičáková-Beblavá, Šípoš and Kurian add at the same time that *"the fastest improvement of score of CPI Slovakia was reached in 2003 to 2007 that corresponds with the commencement of anti-corruption discourse and implementation of anti-corruption reforms."*[22]

Ivan Mikloš in his contribution refers to the difference between the actual levels of corruption and sensibility to corruption by the public what is accepted by academic scholars and publicists. Based on statistics submitted by Mikloš, it is obvious that perception of corruption by the public was increased to a certain point; the number of corruption cases related to the activity of elected representatives of the public slightly dropped; and the number of tried and convicted perpetrators increased. Publicity of corruption in media was simultaneously increased. The number of articles dedicated to the issue of corruption reached only 180 in 1997, and in 2001 there were already 450 articles.[23]

---

20 Školkay, „Strážcovia cností a žurnalistika morálneho rozhorčenia. Investigatívna žurnalistika a jej základné prvky", 81.
21 Sičáková-Beblavá, Šípoš and Kurian, „Korupcia a protikorupčná politika na Slovensku 1989–2010", 166.
22 Ibid., 160.
23 Mikloš, „Správa o boji proti korupcii na Slovensku", 17.

1.2 Slovak Media after 1989

After the revolution in 1989, the society in Slovakia went on a journey of establishing democracy that was based on the model of western world and considered to be a better way of state administration. Its effectiveness was directly proportional to the fact on what tools may be used by the public and media to control the power. According to Kalenborn and Lessmann, democracy has even *"negative influence on the absence of corruption in countries with a low level of freedom of print but it helps to reduce corruption in countries with a high level of media freedom."*[24]

In general, the change of regime stimulated a significant development of media market from the aspect of titles quantity. As Šípoš believes, this boom has two sources whereas both were only temporary. *"Removal of political restrictions opened opportunities on media market what was used by entrepreneurs for business (return of investments) and political purposes (purchase of influence on voters or decision makers). Both were supported by the huge wave of privatization in 90's that generated the class of wealthy entrepreneurs capable of establishing media powers."*[25]

The development of media system was one of the crucial indicators of how the country is successfully able to transform into a state with democratic constitution. The development was characterized by similar circumstances as the fight against corruption described in the previous subchapter. Matúš Minrik in his work from 2000, based on works by Andrej Školkay, describes authoritarian methods used in the era of Vladimír Mečiar's government. *"The list includes changes in legal system, technical obstacles against renewal of the license for public broadcasting, economic pressure, removal of journalists and leading workers of state and public service media and press agency, establishment of own newspapers and magazines, direct and indirect financial support for loyal media, appointing of government supporters to boards of supervisors of public service institutions, refusal of providing information and access to journalists criticizing them, awarding of loyal media or threatening of journalists."*[26] Minárik also referring to

---

24 Kalenborn and Lessmann, The Impact of Democracy and Press Freedom on Corruption: Conditionality Matters, 861.
25 Šípoš, Vlastníctvo médií a jeho dosah na nezávislosť a pluralitu médií, 8.
26 Minárik, Media and Democracy in Slovakia, 14.

Image 2: The Heart of Europe, the Memorial of Velvet Revolution (Author of photo: Miroslava Dobrotková, private archive)

Andrew K. Milton states that *"Slovakia was the only postcommunist country described as immensely difficult place for implementation of new free media in his comparative study of postcommunist countries of middle and Eastern Europe."*[27]

---

27 Ibid., 14.

Insufficient level of freedom of speech and the ability of media to control state officers and politicians has several determining causes. Process by which media transformed after the fall of communism and relating economic influences of leading political powers belongs to crucial ones. In 2004, an analyst Gabriel Šípoš wrote that in Slovakia there was not a uniform scheme of privatization of newspapers." Regardless of this, all print media, however, face strong collision with government political interests – if not during the privatization itself, definitely after it – in the fight for access to distribution and print capacities."[28] Šípoš especially refers to the ability of politicians to push on media through the society that had a monopoly of newspaper distribution and through the owners of printing companies that inclined to the governing People's Party – Movement for a Democratic Slovakia (HZDS) and its leader Vladimír Mečiar. Post newspaper service that had monopoly on press distribution was even half a year before parliamentary elections in 1988 privatized by the Danubiaprint company that was at the same time the biggest printing house in the country and as Šípoš believes controlled by people linked to HZDS. *"Although antimonopoly office declared this transaction invalid at the end of 1998 in the meantime it put pressure on publishers,"* Šípoš states.[29]

During the governments of Mikuláš Dzurinda (from 1998 to 2006) despite the improvement of fight against corruption, analysts did not give a high rating to media regardless of obvious improvement. Although Mečiar's *government* lost elections in 1998, many journalists instinctively kept their liking towards one or another political orientation. *Over the past few years Slovak media begin to avoid party affiliation more and more,"* Šípoš wrote in 2004.[30] An investigative journalist Tom Nicholson spoke about huge pressure on journalists that not necessarily came from the political power three years earlier. *"It comes from two sides: from media owners with political and business motives and from journalists themselves. (…) Journalists face political, economic and social pressure and their work is not precise, free and without the presence of conflict of interests."*[31]

---

28 Šípoš, Vlastníctvo médií a jeho dosah na nezávislosť a pluralitu médií, 2.
29 Šípoš, „Vlastníctvo médií a jeho dosah na nezávislosť a pluralitu médií," 3.
30 Ibid., 8.
31 Nicholson, „Investigatívna žurnalistika na Slovensku: nátlak na zneváženie etiky," 103.

Nicholson also states a case of the daily SME from March 2001 when there was an article on the cover page referring that a businessman Jozef Majský denied suspicion that he threatened his wife with bodily harm if she voted in the favor of constitution. *"Readers did not learn at all what Majský actually said or if he said at least something similar to what he denied,"* says Nicholson.[32] It was the information the daily Plus 7 Dní referred to also without stating a key quote and it was based on assumptions only. *"A SME journalist who took this news from Plus 7 dní later said that it was only a "bubble" produced to draw attention of the public to the cover page."*[33]

Former editor-in-chief of the daily SME and a reputable journalist and publicist Martin M. Šimečka who resigned from his post in 2006 also speaks about the pressures in the daily SME that was considered to be the most serious and independent daily in Slovakia. *"I felt a kind of pressure,"* said Šimečka in 2013 in an interview for the daily SME. He had a dispute with a publisher, but the pressure was initiated by the Prime Minister Mikuláš Dzurinda. "At that time we were defending right-wing reforms of Dzurinda's government regarding comments, but at the same time, we examined their impacts in everyday life of people. *The prime minister Dzurinda and Mikloš were not very excited about. They indirectly pushed on Alexej* (Fulmek the director of the publishing house Petit Press that published the daily – author's note) *to put me right a little bit."*[34] Šimečka added that at that time politicians had influence on the newspaper. *"They had a great influence in economic section, I fired some of the journalists and some of them are back."*[35]

It is paradoxical that this case from 2006 is linked to the most powerful daily SME. Similar information, however, was also sometimes revealed concerning other editorial offices or journalists. In 2011, a recording was disclosed to media where dialogs between the vice-chairman of the opposition party SMER Robert Kaliňák and a journalist from the daily Pravda Vanda Vavrová were captured. In the recording, Kaliňák urges the journalist to write an article about a fast drive of a former minister of defense and

---

32 Ibid., 104.
33 Ibid., 104.
34 Benedikovičová, „Šimečka: SME nehľadá pravdu", online.
35 Ibid., online.

Kaliňák's political rival Ľubomír Galko (Freedom and Solidarity). *"I would like to see those four headlines, baby,"* states the dialog transcription.[36] Based on the transcript, Kaliňák even threatened that he would directly call the daily management.

Similar situation also happened in 2016. A businessman Marián Kočner linked to several economic affairs by media pointed out at anonymous transcripts of text messages and emails between journalists and a political of the New Majority Gábor Grendel in the latest case so far. According to Kočner, anonymously disclosed transcription showed that influential journalists gathered information from Grendel and were influenced by him.[37] Several journalists denied to be influenced by the media, and they found their communication with the politician as a standard one. It is not clear if the transcriptions are credible or modified and where they are from. Several journalists claimed that their reports are real. The case is the subject of an investigation because several journalists lodged a complaint.

Development of media after 1989 also let many media analysts down. One of the most significant one was Samuel Brečka who wrote in 2006 that *"with incoming privatization of media and especially commencement of foreign investors into Slovak media market were many gradually convinced that the freedom of media is the freedom of speech for those who own these media and genuine effort of individuals to fight for the truth and justice collides with insurmountable obstacles caused by those who decide on will or will not be published in media."*[38] Brečka assumes that investigative journalism therefore remained only a theory in Slovakia in 2006.[39] As Brečka states in a research of his team from 2005, only 5% of respondents answered clearly yes to the question "Are journalists independent?" Almost 60% agreed with the answer that only some journalists are independent. *"Based on the results of the research, political pressure on journalists decreased compared with the year of 1997 yet the economic*

---

36 Glovičko, „Kaliňák hovoril redaktorke pravdy, čo má robiť," online.
37 Poláš, „Kočner: Lipšic donášal novinárom. Podľa Grendela je hovorcom Bašternáka", online.
38 Brečka, „Profesia: Novinár", 248.
39 Ibid., 249.

pressure remained very significant felt by 70% of journalists whereas 30% out of them felt the pressure frequently. "[40] Despite described drawbacks, it is indisputable that media system in Slovakia has markedly improved since 1989. Media contributed to solutions of more political or economic affairs, and they are successful in investigating many others. After 23 years of independence, however, under the pressure of globalization, Slovak publishers started to face new challenges and problems. One of the most significant ones was the fall of their revenues (related to economic crisis and development of the Internet) and as a result there is a new wave of ownership concentration. This trend is global and as Dahlgren writes *"journalism and its functions fall into hands of businessmen and managers who have only amateur relationship to traditions and journalism ethics."*[41] Slovak media system reacts on these trends even more sensitively characterized by small market and therefore by limited number of media that can survive on it. Local investors with relative negative reputation resolutely entered into ownership relationships in the system – financial groups Penta and J&T or Slovak tycoon and currently the minister of finance in the Czech Republic Andrej Babiš. For instance, following analysis of INEKO, it is shown that Penta has a quarterly share on the market of dailies (26%) and on the market of weeklies its share reaches up to 65%. Almost one-third share (30%) also belongs to Penta group among news websites on the Internet. Regarding televisions almost one-third (29%) is controlled by J&T group through TV JOJ.[42] Based on these data, it is not demonstrated that Slovak media and their journalists are currently directly influenced by their owners but at the same time historical experience described above leads to carefulness. Its need is underlined by reputation of the mentioned financial groups. Penta group played a crucial role in Gorilla scandal; J&T group was present at energetic scandals or scandals concerning highway toll or conversion course of Slovak koruna. Both groups regarding their business activity often meet with state activities of regulated sectors such as health care (Penta) or energetics (J&T). It is, therefore, logical that they care about the form and amendments of

---

40 Ibid., 249.
41 Dahlgren, "The transformation of Democracy?", 70.
42 Galmišová, Kauzám sa najviac venujú v denníku SME, 19–23.

legislation in these sectors to potentially secure the tools to influence or lessen their regulations. One of the establishing partners of the financial group Penta directly said that investment into the media group is not autotelic but it is a hot way to protect their business. *"I will not beat about the bush. The fact we own the media provides us with a certainty that for anyone it would be more difficult to attack us irrationally."*[43]

In 2014, a substantial part of the editorial office of the daily SME left and founded a new media Denník N as a protest of this investor's entry to the ownership structure of the most powerful daily at that time. Former editor-in-chief of SME daily and currently the editor-in-chief of Denník N daily, Matúš Kostolný, together with his representatives explained their decision in a detailed statement.

Among other things, they wrote that *"Penta does not behave as a standard investor who wants to do business in media to make profit out of his readers and advertising. Excessively high price offered to Petit Press also proves that Penta was especially interested in the influence of SME brand name. If we had stayed in SME under these circumstances we would have nodded to the game in which media do not care about the interests of its readers but they are a power tool of its owners, too."*[44]

1.3 Results of Slovak Media in the Power Control

One of the crucial questions opened by the theoretical framework interpreted in the previous text is the current state and performance of Slovak media in the power control in comparison with the past. In general, the development of media environment in Slovakia since 1989 has been divided into the period of already-mentioned mečiarizmus (Vladimír Mečiar's government) with its significant features such as restricting of freedom and power control and subsequent freeing. Based on this division, the following research with respect to limits of the database compares the volume and character of news reports in 1999 and 2015. Besides our own research, two current studies will also serve as the basis for answering this question – from the

---

43 Mikulka, „Spolumajiteľ Penty Dospiva: Chceme mediální štít proti iracionálním útokům.", online.
44 Kostolný, „Prečo odchádzame z denníka SME", online.

DENNÍK N

Pôvodný dočasný blog autorov Denníka N.

✉ f 🐦

Prečo odchádzame z denníka SME

Štyri citáty namiesto úvodu

„Je mi jedno, či niekto pracoval pre CIA alebo KGB, či bol členom ústredného výboru alebo disident. Pokiaľ je človek šikovný a uznávaný vo svojej brandži, nič iné ma nezaujíma."

Týmto výrokom Jaroslav Haščák v minulosti obhajoval zamestnávanie bývalého šéfa komunistickej Štátnej bezpečnosti Alojza Lorenca, ale je formulovaná širšie, ako jeho obchodná a životná filozofia. Denník SME vždy zastával opačný názor - že nie je jedno, kde ľudia pracujú a videl rozdiel v tom, či sa niekto stal úspešným vďaka vlastnej šikovnosti, alebo vďaka utláčaniu či okrádaniu iných. Vyrovnávanie sa s fašistickou, komunistickou aj mečiarovskou minulosťou boli vždy veľké témy týchto novín, podobne ako obhajoba ľudských práv.

„Prirodzene, že nám záleží na tom, aké legislatívne prostredie na Slovensku bude. V tomto kontexte sme aktívni, keďže politické rozhodnutia sa dotýkajú nielen nás, ale aj zamestnancov, ktorí pracujú v spoločnostiach v rámci našej skupiny."

Image 3: Print screen of the website created in 2014 with the statement of Matúš Kostolný (http://www.opentat.sk/post/99715656100/ pre%C4%8Do-odch%C3%A1dzame-z-denn%C3%ADka-sme)

Czech media analyst and academic scholar Václav Štětka and from Slovak non-governmental institute INEKO.

The research was conducted following the model of already-mentioned work by Václav Štětka by selection of discourses based on a key word. In regard to the subject and character of the research as well as to the pre-research, a word *"scandal"* was selected as a key word that generated sufficient amount of data in the research period from 1 January to 31 December of both the years. This selected research sample was further specified by connecting the key word to a representative of the state respectively – public power and publishing of information about the facts of the case in the two media, at least what ensured the relevance of the topic. All the universal influential nationwide dailies, still published nowadays, such as SME, Pravda and Hospodárske noviny (at that time in Slovakia besides tabloid, specialized and sports dailies were dailies such as Slovenská republika, Národná obroda and Hospodársky denník that are no longer published) were the source of data from 1999. Web portals of the mentioned dailies and a new project Denník N were involved in the research in 2016. Such selected discourses were further classified into four groups based on their dependence on intelligence value of new information brought by discourse.

Work limits: While comparing the quality of information, it is necessary to take into consideration the fact that more dailies from 1999 do not exist and on the contrary informatization of the society enables new possibilities of cheap and effective spreading of information on the Internet resulting in the establishment of plenty more- or less-quality media. Although these media are not involved in the research (except for Denník N), their work may influence results of the research. On one hand, themes open to these either ceased or new media could also be an impulse for the researched media to focus on some topics, and on the other hand, the overall number of topics open by media in both the years could be higher than captured in the research mainly due to existence of two other communication channels. Newly established Internet media without a print title in the background, however, do not produce substantial amount of unique topics; they rather focus on publishing news from newswire, social networks or information taken from other media despite their slowly changing character.

Such conceived research indicated that media nowadays are more effective than they were in 1999 in regard to power control. The overall number of discourses corresponding with the key word increased in the research period in absolute numbers by more than one thousand, what represents 180%. The number of relevant results based on the specification of research sample increased by 152%. Simultaneously, much more topics were involved in the public space within one year. Eleven topics appeared in research journals in 1999, and in 2015 there were 40 topics. These data do not necessarily mean that media nowadays are able to control larger amount of decisions and steps taken by representatives of the state power.

It is demonstrated in the statistics of topics open by media in this particular year. Based on the data analyzed in 1999, it is possible to say that the topic was open by one particular medium concerning only one topic – it was the case of state testing institute Hospodársky noviny (HN). In comparison to one topic in 1999, the year 2015 was a little richer in topics open by media. Based on the data analyzed, three of them may be specifically determined whereas the daily SME informed about two of them and Hospodárske noviny about one of the cases. The ratio 1:3 almost exactly corresponds to the ratio in the absolute number of articles selected based on a key word. If we perceive the ratio of open topics through the prism of absolute numbers, they are so low that it is not relevant to deduce significant increase of performance of media from them in the field of opening their own new affairs.

Moreover, this issue contains several significant variables not involved in the submitted research. One of the most important is the duration of corruption scandals. In 1999, media in majority of cases were engaged in topics concerning the privatization of state property rooted deeply before 1999. The result of the research therefore does not mean that media did not open these topics but that they did not open them in this specific year, yet they could have done so in the past. On the other hand, at present, the course and duration of corruption cases are much shorter which is connected with the speed of information flow. In regard to the number of relevant topics in public discussion in the individual years (11:40), it may be additionally said that in a public space, the space provided for topics is four times more compared to the past.

A similar research was conducted by a colleague from the institute INEKO Dominika Galmišová at the turn of 2014 and 2015.[45] The subject of the research was the number of articles dedicated to individual news media concerning ten selected cases and how many of them they opened themselves. The most successful was the daily SME with its web portal sme.sk. In total, they opened seven out of ten cases and also informed about them the most (almost up to one-fifth of the articles of the followed scandals belongs to the daily SME and its Internet variant). Besides SME, its own case was only opened by the weekly Plus 7 Dní and TV Markíza

---

45 Galmišová, Kauzám sa najviac venujú v denníku SME, 1–23.

together with SME informing about one scandal (CT scan device). Public service RTVS informed about the scandals the most in comparison to other televisions. Galmišová collected but did not further analyze data related to preference of print and web platform of individual media, respectively. In all the seven cases, the first article marked as scandal opening by Galmišová was first published online regarding SME that had a dominant position in the research. This fact may be important for deciding the question if effective power control really requires survival of print dailies. There are not enough data in the study for proving a clear conclusion. In case of all five followed dailies (SME, HN, Pravda, Plus 1 deň, Nový Čas) they dedicated more time for scandals online rather than in print. The research did not deal with the value and authenticity of individual articles.

A Czech academic scholar Václav Štětka in his research from 2012 monitored the influence of scandals revealed by journalists on the public and taking political responsibility. In his research, he compared data from the counties of middle and Eastern Europe – Bulgaria, the Czech Republic, Estonia, Hungary, Latvia, Lithuania, Poland, Romania and Slovakia. He was interested in the fact about how many office workers or politicians resigned in these individual countries from 2007 to 2011 after revealing a corruption scandal in media. The biggest success was reached by media in Estonia where on average seven office workers resigned annually. Vice versa, the least number (one on average) resigned in Bulgaria. Slovakia had an average of 3.5 resigned office workers per year. Compared with a competition of eight countries, it is in the third place. Štětka objectified these results and interpreted them through interviews with investigative journalists from the mentioned countries.

Based on the research, the ratio of resigned or even convicted office workers is still relatively low compared to the Western world. *"Respondents in their interviews often put an emphasis on the fact that office workers who were accused of corruption often remained in their offices regardless of media pressure or they temporarily retired until the media pressure moved elsewhere."*[46]As Štětka believes, the number of convicted office workers

---

46　Štětka, "The watchdogs that only bark? Media and political accountability in Central and Eastern Europe", 8.

Image 4: The gray building in the middle of the photo is one of the headquarters of the Slovak company and finance group J&T and of the JOJ Television. The logos of companies originally set on the top of the building were digitally removed. (Author of photo: Miroslava Dobrotková, private archive)

even highlights the skepticism. *"In many countries, an office worker is rarely convicted no matter if he is forced to resign and the legal proceedings has been commenced against him."*[47] In majority of monitored countries, it was one person within five years covered in the study. Poland was an exception with three representatives of power convicted. Moreover, Štětka emphasized that the system works in a paradoxical way at first sight. In countries where the level of perceived corruption is the highest, investigative journalism has the lowest effect. The author placed Slovakia into this category alongside Bulgaria and Romania.[48]

---

47 Ibid., 8.
48 Ibid., 8.

Image 5: One of the headquarters of Slovak company ESET. The logos of companies originally set on the top of the building were digitally removed. (Author of photo: Miroslava Dobrotková, private archive)

1.4 Summary

Slovak media system within a relatively short period of time of its independent development experienced several turbulences, periods of quality increase as well as moments of crisis undermining its trust. It is indisputable that Slovak media nowadays are on the highest level ever. It is much more difficult to answer the questions if it is sufficient, if they perform their function properly and if they do not have an adequate level of trust. Not only quality of media changes but the society, technologies and the level of interaction in horizontal and vertical plane evolve in time. Nowadays, there is no clear answer to these asked questions. From the philosophical point of view, the society has such media as it deserves, respectively journalists are also only members of certain society that creates the state and the world around us. Such a general definition, however, is not sufficient for media nowadays. They need to search for models how to improve their work quality and how to gain trust of the public as well as resources for material security of increasing quality without becoming vassals of their owners or sponsors.

At present, several media show their interest to search for other ways and to risk to become different, more attractive and most read or watched media. It is often at the expense of bulvarization, yet several media try charging of their content that they experiment with applications or new Internet formats. Signs of inter-editorial cooperation, deeper investigative work and eventually public pressure on transparency of public administration may be found. As presented research as well as older data of Ivan Mikloš showed the volume of articles about corruption and slips of power, anti-corruption measures together with the availability of media are still on the rise. All of these serve as a good base for further development of watchdog journalism. Another important step indicated by the research of Václav Štětka is to make the work of investigative journalist provide results not only in the form of published discourses but also in the form of subsequent pressure on solving problems and taking responsibility against those whose misconduct is proved. Several analysts, publicist and also journalists find it as a reason for frustration of the public and its relative weak ability to mobilize itself.

2 Current Issues of Presenting of Stereotypes in Mass Media
(Influence of Media on Presenting of Stereotypes and Prejudice within Political Communication and Its Correlation with Perception through the Web)

Stereotypes and prejudices in the society are not a problem nowadays – they have existed as long as the humankind itself. Their presentation in media appears since their beginning either due to political affiliation, propaganda or bulvarization of media content. Their presentation and communication on the Internet, as it will be shown, became a current and very considerable issue in the recent years and uncovered negative emotions in the society to a much greater extent.

At present, especially due to repeated increase of nationalist and extremist moods in the society, there is a need for rational and human judgment based on analysis of facts and social needs. As we believe, the objective of society actions should be the search for successful forms of social and cultural integration of social minorities.

2.1 Influence of Media Concerning Integration of Social Minorities

A professor Geissler considers *"unity in diversity"* – intercultural integration as the fundamental principle of cultural integration. It is not multiculturalism but a sort of living abreast without any effort for coexistence but integration with an emphasis on the common and on exchange of cultural determinateness built on establishing common rules, common language and common social values with equal chances for participation in certain spheres of life and active acceptation by majority society.[49]

Local knowledge is, however, not sufficient in regard to an effort for integration in global society. Without sufficient knowledge of social, political, economic and cultural connections, it is not possible to appraise social

---

49 Geissler, „Mediale Integration von ethnischen Minderheiten", 5.

events based only on experience made by immediate contact. Especially media has its importance while creating images and opinions from an environment independent from knowledge.[50] Percipients meet with events not happening in their environment and expand their knowledge in experience of life of social minorities and migrants through them. An individual, without personal experience, living in close proximity of the group of non-integrated persons cannot imagine that representatives of the minority may have a university degree, may be integrated and beneficial for society. According to Rosinský, whose results were based on nationwide research, 726 members of Romani ethnicity have university diploma, and in 2013, it is estimated that about 486 Romani students were obtaining it.[51] Successful Romani may be found among artists, sportsmen, journalists, regional politician, etc. Despite this fact, there are prejudice and stereotypes in the society against this ethnicity.

Based on the research focused on the image of the Romani in Slovak media conducted by an organization Romano Khers in 2014 in Slovakia, the most common stereotypes in media are as follows:

a) about criminality: they steal more than majority;
b) social: they are dependent on social benefits and have many children; they are not able to provide their accommodation;
c) work: they are lazy and not interested in looking for a job;
d) educational: they study less and are not intelligent enough;
e) hygienic: they do not have hygienic habits;
f) stereotypes about living: they are not able to provide their own accommodation; they destroy what is given to them.[52]

The Romani are depicted as an anonymous group. If necessary, media address almost exclusively Romani plenipotentiary – as the representative of elites. Voices of professionals and figures from the ethnicity environment specialized in Romani issue are missing.[53]

---

50 Thomson, Média a modernita, 168.
51 Rosinský, „Rómovia v číslach na Slovensku a v Nitrianskom kraji", 99.
52 Newton media, Mediálna analýza pre Romano Kher – Rómsky dom: 1. júl–31. október 2016, 14.
53 Newton media, Rómovia, novinári a médiá: Mediálna analýza: 1. Júl–30. November 2014, 9.

In times of increasing prejudices, stereotypes, fear and refusal of seeking solutions media influence not only what society is supposed to know and what they should think about it but especially how to think of the given situation.[54] Although prejudice and stereotypes of social groups living beyond our personal experience are not created by media only but also by so-called opinion leaders,- media may strengthen them and issue of social, political and cultural diversity simplify and generalize. Politicians are also adopting to this based on purely pragmatic reasons.

While depicting reality, media are influenced by their value orientation and in case of tabloid and commercial media preferred by percipients especially inclination to emotionalism, negativism, controversy and to elites.[55] However, it is not to professionals from the fields of sociology, culturology, ethnology and politics but to so-called elites from the environment of political parties and to individuals whose statements provoke controversy and emotions. As an analysis on the image of Romani in Slovak media, stated professionals and figures from the environment of ethnic minority are represented by politicians and office workers.[56]

Various forms of manipulation, staging, marginalization of alternatives and other opinions, infotainment, emotionalism, bulvarization of politics and simplification of complicated political decisions belong to negative influences of media. Examples of manipulation in Slovak media are stated in a contribution by Lincényi and Tamene.[57]

2.2 Influence of Media and the Internet on Politics and Political Communication

Politicians and political parties are also aware of this fact, and in regard to their campaigns, they employ professionals in media including so-called

---

54 Krejčí, Politická psychologie, 129.
55 Schultz, Politische Kommunikation. Theoretische Ansätze und Ergebnisse empirischer Forschung zur Rolle in der Politik, 66–70 a 88–100. and Veverková, Bulvár a bulvarizácia dennej tlače, 70–72.
56 Newton media, Rómovia, novinári a médiá: Mediálna analýza: 1. Júl–30. November 2014, 1–23.
57 Lincényi and Tamene, "The media as public opinion leader in influencing and setting policy: the case of Slovakia", 95–99.

media planning. They analyze media, their philosophy, program and orientation, and they are surveying what forms of presentation in media and on the Internet resonate the most.

Media are very important means of influencing the public for both politicians and aspiring politicians. As professor Krejči emphasizes, the interest of public in political topics is created by mass media that determine *"what meaning is ascribed to politics – they tune the image of politics up (...) and determine the way how residents decide on what is important in politics (...) and decide on how alternatives will be perceived by residents – they prefer selected options."*[58]

According to Meyer, the author of mediocracy, this fact has a real impact on democracy. Politicians try to adapt their decisions and political programs to logics of media. There is a change of roles: In party democracy, the role of media is to follow politics and help the public to create their own sensible opinion. In media democracy, political participants analyze media system to adapt their decisions and way of presentation to them.[59]

As Polakevičová states in her contribution, the relationship between voters and political subjects has recently become rather exchangeable and political candidates are presented there as the subjects of business.[60] A voter chooses political party as a life insurance; unfortunately, it is not often based on its actual program but based on its cover.

Although the influence of media on decisions of percipients in elections was not that important, there are doubts regarding success of media-attractive politicians with controversial background. Politicians who did not reach their status by career progression linked to their loyalty towards to the party, erudition in a particular field and political education but only by popularity gained by their presentation in media, use media-attractive ways of presentation for gaining the space: drama, emotion, storiness, theatralization-political staging.[61] Gradually, (maybe also based on media and electoral success of these politicians) political representatives of standard

---

58 Krejčí, Politická psychologie, 129.
59 Meyer, „Die Theatralität der Politik in der Mediendemokratie", 12.
60 Polakevičová, "Controversy of media discourses in (A)political campaigns to referendum for protection of family 2015 in media space in Slovakia", 11–19.
61 Napr. Meyer, „Die Theatralität der Politik in der Mediendemokratie", 12–19.

political parties adapted by their performing and form of communication who have equally as some media tendency to strengthen stereotypes and prejudices in society.

As the form of media staging based on our topic of strengthening of stereotypes and prejudice, for example, involve:

a) organization of press conference of traditional former governmental political party SDKÚ in illegal buildings in a Romani settlement.[62] Despite the fact that attractive interesting buildings for media without necessary permission may be found among houses of majority population as well;

b) organization promoting a neo-Nazi Marián Kotleba who was neither a member of the National Council of the Slovak Republic nor the chairman of Banská Bystrica Self-Governing Region in a Romani settlement Krásna Hôrka as *"savior"* of interests of responsible people.[63] Let's say that it was publicity of his society-unfriendly actions when he was not a politician, and his steps were not necessarily to be publicized that markedly contributed to his election to all stated offices.

The problem we stated has been strengthened by the possibility of online discussion in recent years. Although in its first years of existence, some theoreticians excitedly assumed positive influence of the Internet on change of politics from a purely spectator to participatory one,[64] others pointed out at the information gap created by percipients themselves by narrowing of the choice of suitable sources of information and by creating small groups that encourage each other in their opinions censoring other information and ridiculing those with different opinions.[65] As psychologist Vybíral says: *"What used to be hidden is now displayed."*[66] Losing all inhibitions and scruples, the loss of shyness, bashfulness and timidity, relaxedness

---

62 SITA, „Frešo chce búrať osady a čierne stavby", online.

63 PK, „Kotleba dostal pozemky pod Krásnou Hôrkou", online; and TASR (Tlačová agentúra Slovenskej republiky), „Kotleba považuje domy Rómov za odpad, ktorý chce zlikvidovať", online.

64 Leggewie, „Demokratie auf der datenautobahn", 15–54.

65 Jakubowicz, „Nová média a demoracie", 223–270; and Noam, „Digitaler Schwindel"

66 Vybíral, Psychologie komunikace, 272–274.

or non-binding of norms may even reach abnormal size.[67] We do not say that the Internet causes gradation of racism. Aggressive manifestation of racism and xenophobia was there before its existence. The Internet, however, made its manifestations more visible, materialized and spread them among people who might not have been influenced by it and encouraged them in their thinking.

The Internet simultaneously became one of the means (not only) of political marketing. Politicians use it to present their political programs, attitudes and opinions; they express themselves in regard to social, political situation and to information from media and media vice versa follow conversations of politicians on the Internet that is based on their philosophy – bulvarization, emotionalism, storiness and negativity – they process and share it online to their percipients who subsequently discuss a politician's opinion. Spiral of publicizing (in our case) of stereotypes and prejudice gains its momentum.

2.3 Reasons for Combination of Forms of Analysis

We find insufficient to analyze presentation of social phenomena without their correlation with the form of presentation on so-called social networks and in discussion at times of internetization of media and society especially due to the possibility of perception of media texts nowadays and in cooperation with discussion which complete content respectively text impression. The form of a media text nowadays does not end with its publication, especially due to potential gradation of society-unfriendly reactions and disinhibition.

In our contribution, we analyze the influence of media on forms of presentation of prejudice and stereotypes in the communication of politicians, their finishing and the way of promoting through the web and subsequent gradation within discussion on online discussion forums. Using the analysis of discourse and conversation analysis of particular cases of the performance of politicians in media, we present the relationship of journalists, politicians and the public to negativization and emotionalism of information, disinhibition and strengthening of prejudice and stereotypes.

---

67 Ibid., 272–274.

We analyze media texts and their mutual correlation through analysis of a discourse. For analysis of their sharing and communication via the Internet, we chose conversation analysis.

In the period of internetization of media, especially in regard to emotionally tense information, we find using of standard discourse analysis insufficient. Discourse analysis does not allow analysis of forms of mutual connection, sharing and communicating of information by various users using communication networks.

Although the form of presentation of information as well as subsequent analysis on Internet forums regarding its emotionalism, language means being used and so-called emoticons approaches to a standard discussion, we find conversation analysis more suitable.

Discourse analysis is focused on institutionalized and professional procedures of communication where topic and sphere are especially important. *"Genre of discourse, their style and vocabulary is analyzed. Detailed analysis of expressions used, grammar forms and rhetoric figures are carried out within them."*[68] Conversation analysis focuses on structural problem of communication it attempts to solve. It is understood as analysis of structure and interaction.[69]

We apply discourse analysis on analysis of media performances and Internet statuses, and conversation analysis on analysis of discussion on the Internet in regard to the issue we research.

Internet discussion concerning their content and extent may be compared to standard discussion, and therefore we believe that we may analyze them using conversation analysis.

Manifestations of emotions are replaced with using so-called emoticons – a pictorial representation of emotions by discussants in written speech. Angriness is emphasized by using exclamation marks, puzzlement by question marks and louder voice by using capital letters.

Although the Internet discussion is presented in a written form, it approaches standard conversation by frequent usage of grammatical and

---

68 Vávra, „Tři přístupy k analýze diskurzu – neslučitelnost nebo možnost syntézy?", 53.
69 Galinski, „Zweierlei Perspektiven auf Gespräche: Ethnomethodologische Konversationsanalyse und Diskursanalyse in kontrastiven Vergleich", 22–23.

Image 6: The discussion program broadcasted by RTVS (public broadcaster) on 21/01/2018 (http://www.rtvs.sk/televizia/archiv/13004/145992, online)

stylistic mistakes that may be a result of either low education of discussants or fast speed of their careless responding, what is again typical for live conversation.

2.4 Analysis of a Particular Example

We chose the status of a deputy of the National Council of the Slovak Republic and the chairman of political party "We are family" Boris Kollár on Facebook social network where he shared an article about integration of Romani children into standard elementary school of May, 2016 for analysis of a particular example of influence of media on presentation of stereotypes and prejudice within political communication and their correlation with perception through the web.

The reason for choice of the analyzed case is especially the way of presentation which, based on analysis of subsequent discussion, may be perceived as encouraging stereotypes and prejudices.

Boris Kollár is the chairman of a relatively new political party "We are family" established shortly before elections in 2016. Within the efforts of the society to integrate and accept migrants and Romani, he acts as a critic and a person who encourages prejudice and stereotypes in the media and on the Internet.

On his Facebook fan page on 15 May 2015, he posted a status where he shared an article by online newspaper Hlavné správy[70] criticizing proposals of Slovak Governance Institute for gradual inclusion of children from socially disadvantaged environment to standard schools.

2.5 Original Document of Slovak Governance Institute

To be able to state non-objectiveness and bias of the authors of media performances, statuses and discussion contributions, we need to state information from the original document of Slovak Governance Institute within our analysis.[71]

A reviewed publication prepared by a team of ten practitioners is based on analysis and correlation of problems from the field of children education from socially disadvantaged environment; partial results were validated and supplemented by results from discussion with professional public. In its publication of 150 pages, it assesses the facts and proposes specific steps to *"increase chances from socially disadvantaged environment without other special educational needs to succeed in standard elementary school and gradually provide education of children with less serious special educational needs in main educational flow."*[72]

The authors proposed gradual improvement of diagnostics of children regarding their inclusion in special elementary schools, making of transit classes within special elementary schools for children who have prerequisites to get to standard elementary schools and to provide them with education at standard high schools, improvement of pre-elementary education, increasing of availability of zero grades at elementary schools

---

70 Internet portal that presents itself as an alternative conservative daily and that is criticized especially for biased pro-Russian news service and seditious vocabulary. (Šnídl, V. „Kto riadi proruský web Hlavné správy? Muž, ktorý odmieta eurofondy", online.)

71 Farenzenová, Kubánová and Salner, Cestovná mapa pre riešenie problému nadmerného zastúpenia rómskych detí v špeciálnom školstve – analýza realistických krokov, 1–150.

72 Ibid., 99.

and increasing of interest of parents and children in educating their children in standard schools. Proposed particular steps, needs and requirements including evaluation of costs until 2025 were a part of the publication. In the conclusion of the report, the author states that non-solving of this issue is not only against human-right requirements of the society but it may influence performance of economy and prosperity of the society in the future.[73]

As it results from the following analysis of the article, status and discussion posts none of the people criticizing read the study – neither the author of the article nor discussants – and nobody made an effort to find original information, so everyone was happy with the information from the published article and politician's status.

The report of PISA 2012 in which Slovakia was placed among countries where the influence of social-economic background on education is significantly higher than the average of OECD (Organisation for Economic Co-operation and Development),[74] countries informed about the need for seeking solution of the problem mentioned.

One of the authors of the publication of Slovak Governance Institute, Martina Kubánová, published a commentary on 17 April 2016 in the daily SME where she stated an excessive number of children in special schools and ineligibility of representation of excessive number of Roma children what, as she assumes, prevent them from integration in society, and among other things she proposes *"to transform special elementary school into standard schools with standard and special classes under the administration of municipality (in 2008, similar step was taken by regional school office for instance in case of ŠZŠ in Telgárt and ŠZŠ in Poltár in the Banská Bystrica region which were abolished and their students joined an elementary school with special classes in these municipalities)."*[75]

The mentioned commentary probably became the only source of information that subsequently lead to other misinterpretations and attacks. Our assumption is based on the fact that the author of the analyzed article

---

73 Ibid., 99–135.
74 OECD, PISA 2012 Results in Focus: What 15-year-olds know and what they can do with What they know, 13.
75 Kubánová, „Keď jediná škola v obci je len pre mentálne postihnuté deti", online.

cited only the author of the commentary as a submitter of proposals and amendments and not the entire team of Slovak Governance Institute.

2.6 Discourse Analysis of the Article and Politician's Status

The analyzed article *"European Commission and Non-Governmental Organization Propose for Inclusion of Special Schools with Romani Falling Behind with Standard Schools,"*[76] was published on a portal hlavnespravy. sk on 15 May 2016 which is almost one month after Kubánová's commentary was published.

The author confirms stereotypes about mental and educational retardation of Romani ethnicity already in the headline when he assumes that special schools are attended only by members of Romani ethnicity.

In the following text, the author of the article paraphrases proposals of Slovak Governance Institute that proposes to include special classes in standard schools. They are supposed to function *alongside* standard classes. Author subsequently interprets such an outlined proposal based on his own judgment *"it raised question if such inclusion of special classes in standard schools would not cause disturbance in educational process for all children."*[77] Later he informs about attempts to gradually transform special schools into standard schools with special and standard classes to prevent spatial segregation of Romani children. Specification of an employee of the institute that it refers to 19 municipalities with not solely Romani population the author called *"a sloppy method to lull the public"*,[78] and potential possibility to gradually integrate all special classes in standard schools in this way (without their inclusion with standard classes), the authors find it as a threat. The fact that it is supposed to be integration of special respectively transit classes into standard schools by their maintaining that would allow ordinary children to meet children requiring another approach and to socialize and humanize them is on the contrary not allowed. At the same

---

76 TASR and Kapusta, „Európska komisia a mimovládna organizácia navrhujú
    zlúčiť špeciálne školy so zaostávajúcimi Rómami s bežnými školami", online.
77 Ibid., online.
78 Ibid., online.

time, it definitely results from the text that the author did not attempt to find out the original source of the proposals.

The report does not meet standards set on news service such as informativeness, objectiveness and impartiality and either publicist genres as commentary and analysis that are supposed to compare various opinions, proposals and their analysis and assessment.

The author of the article does not specify parts of criticism of the European Commission he states in the introduction not supporting criticism of institution in any way. Within dialoged net, the author of the article quotes only the author of the commentary indirectly addressing her in this way. Statements of other professionals concerning this topic attempt to integration in elementary schools, and their results are missing. The article is very subjective with clear intention to support reader's prejudices against Romani population, children in special schools and their school integration. The author of the article does not doubt his own prejudices. Besides prejudice against non-educational level of Romani and by no means supported criticism of the European Commission, however, the author did not refrain from other stereotypical characteristics.

Much more prejudices and stereotypes may be found in a status of a deputy of the Slovak National Council of the Slovak Republic Boris Kollár who shared the analyzed article the same day it was published. He called children from special classes *"retarded, many times demented,"* Romani children from settlements as *"pretty retarded"* and people trying for their integration *"idiots who want to push them into normal healthy children."* Similarly, the author of the article assumes that the intention of the authors will lower the level of education and possibility of application of children from standard schools. In the conclusion, in brackets, he states that his criticism does not involve smart Romani children but students *"of the level of special school, simple retarded children,"* and he assumes that by similar decisions the authors may cause financial burden of *"white families"* and *"achieving greater hatred towards Gypsies."*[79] Similarly as the author of the article, he does not doubt his prejudices, does not try to understand its

---

79 Boris Kollár's Facebook page, accessed January 25, 2017, https://www.facebook. com/permalink.php?story_fbid=1614954265492309&id=1464024763918594.

intention and does not argue. He ignores the absence of original source of information in the shared article what leads to its greater misinterpretation.

Ethical principles of journalism as it is in media do not involve personal Internet websites and statutes on social websites. Behavior of politicians in public is determined especially by their intellectual and moral level. The way of their behavior, however, becomes the model of behavior for the public.

Neither the author of the article nor the politician makes an effort for seeking respectively offer when solving problems of social integration of social excluded children. They simplify, attack and criticize proposals of professionals – strengthening prejudices and stereotypes of their percipients.

Although the shared article contains prejudices and stereotypes against Romani population and children from special schools, in politician's status and discussion posts, we noticed that 468 (332 direct reactions and 136 replies) greatly intensify by their number and power.

2.7 Conversion Analysis of Discussion on Facebook

As we already mentioned below the post of Boris Kollár, we noticed 468 discussion posts. Many of them showed stereotypes and prejudices against Romani as assumptions that children in special schools are asocial and that bullying, aggressiveness and humiliation will be automatically increased in standard schools[80] that opponents of school integration and inclusion are families "with normal moral principles"[81] blaming Romani for incest that would "not allow to receive any (social) benefits!",[82] requiring to stop giving birth (…) as lice"[83]respectively as

---

80 Comment on Boris Kollár's Facebook page, May 15, *2016* (11:20 a.m.) accessed January 25, 2017, https://www.facebook.com/permalink.php?story_fbid=1614954265492309&id=1464024763918594.

81 Comment on Boris Kollár's Facebook page, May 15, 2016 (11:19 a.m.), accessed January 25, 2017, https://www.facebook.com/permalink.php?story_fbid=1614954265492309&id=1464024763918594.

82 Comment on Boris Kollár's Facebook page, May 15, 2016 (10:51 a.m.), accessed January 25, 2017, https://www.facebook.com/permalink.php?story_fbid=1614954265492309&id=1464024763918594.

83 Comment on Boris Kollár's Facebook page, May 16, 2016 (10:34 a.m.), accessed January 25, 2017, https://www.facebook.com/permalink.php?story_fbid=1614954265492309&id=1464024763918594.

rats,[84] assuming that "hepatitis, stink and mess at school will be in standard regime",[85] using stereotypes and prejudices about parasitizing on social system[86] accusing the society of "genocide of white men"[87] and smashing the nation by Romani, Arabs and "retarded ones" with an intention to make people stupid.[88]

Posts related to politician's statement either verbal or by using of emoticon with raised thumb may belong to discuss posts with inappropriate content. We counted 433 of them in discussions in total. Only 35 posts criticizing presented opinion of Boris Kollár what refers to 7.5% of posts in total.

Information from original report disappeared from reactions of discussants. Stereotypes, prejudices, fear and affirmative reactions to politician's opinion prevailed. Authors of the posts were satisfied with the current situation in education. They agreed in their mutual reactions regardless of some exceptions, and they supported each other's prejudices. Although we did not find inhumane solution of problems in the discussion.

There were also posts where discussants argued with each other. *"Are we birds of a feather that you are on first-name terms with me?"*[89] or they contradicted each other: K.H-B.: *"I live in Austria and integration schools*

---

84 Comment on Boris Kollár's Facebook page, May 16, 2016 (6:20 a.m.), accessed January 25, 2017, https://www.facebook.com/permalink.php?story_fbid=1614 954265492309&id=1464024763918594.

85 Comment on Boris Kollár's Facebook page, May 16, 2016 (3:24 p.m.), accessed January 25, 2017, https://www.facebook.com/permalink.php?story_fbid=1614 954265492309&id=1464024763918594.

86 Comment on Boris Kollár's Facebook page, May 16, 2016 (11:42 a.m.), accessed January 25, 2017, https://www.facebook.com/permalink.php?story_fbid=1614 954265492309&id=1464024763918594.

87 Comment on Boris Kollár's Facebook page, May 16, 2016 (7:37 a.m.), accessed January 25, 2017, https://www.facebook.com/permalink.php?story_fbid=1614 954265492309&id=1464024763918594.

88 Comment on Boris Kollár's Facebook page, May 16, 2016 (8:40 a.m.), accessed January 25, 2017, https://www.facebook.com/permalink.php?story_fbid=1614 954265492309&id=1464024763918594.

89 Comment on Boris Kollár's Facebook page, May 16, 2016 (1:57 p.m.)–May 17, 2016 (10:00 a.m.), accessed January 25, 2017, https://www.facebook.com/ permalink.php?story_fbid=1614954265492309&id=1464024763918594.

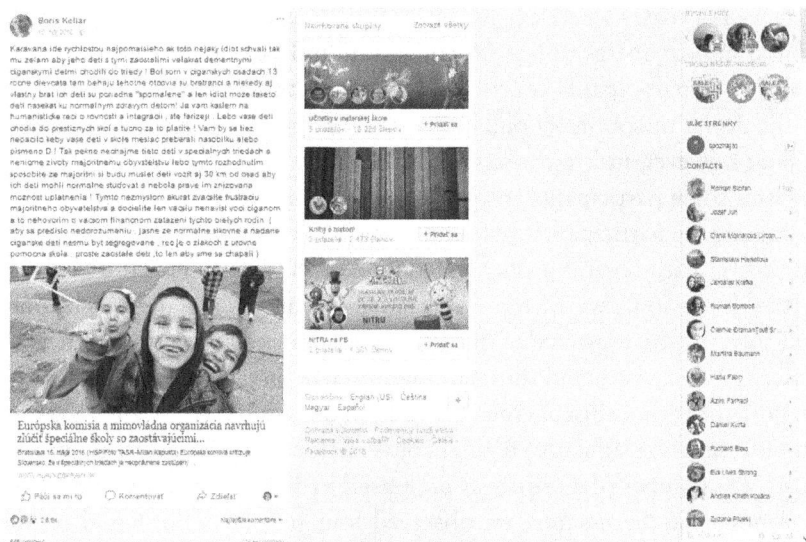

Image 7: Status of Boris Kollár (Slovak politician), in which the author spreads the stereotypes and prejudices against the Roma ethnic group by disinterpreting the proposals of the Slovak Governance Institute for the integration of Roma children in their education. (Boris Kollár, 2016, online)

function very well in here… (10:02 a.m.) K.: But we are in Slovakia (10:16 a.m.) M.T.: And especially years behind the times (10:18 a.m.) K. H-B.: I'm so sorry… If we could organize it this way in Slovakia it would be great! (10:32 a.m.) M.C.: Nor in Austria they integrated its just a false image…a gloss that it works but in practice…nooo way (10:57 a.m.) N.H.: Boris there will be ROCK n ROLL" For God's sake where does it all lead! (12:03 p.m.) K.L.: What K.H-B. writes could work somewhere in Bratislava where the intelligence level even of those asocial individuals is higher, standard of living, too… (12:28 p.m.) J. H-B.: M.C., my daughter attended such integration class. It really worked…" (01:32 p.m.)[90]

---

90 Comment on Boris Kollár's Facebook page, May 16, 2016 (10:02 a.m.–01:32 p.m.), accessed January 25, 2017, https://www.facebook.com/permalink. php?story_fbid=1614954265492309&id=1464024763918594.

Especially cases where discussants talk to each other in an online discussion, it approximates to regular conversation. In the analyzed discussion, majority of participants contributed by one or two posts, which may lead to the doubt of confusing online discussions with regular conversation or dialog; however, in live discussion, especially when more participants are present, some participants comment on the topic only once or twice.

Among the participants we found those who contributed to the analyzed discussion with several posts. The author of the status replied nine times in the discussion, two of the most active opponents six and seven times and three of the most active discussants who agreed with the politician's statement five, seven and thirteen times. Active discussants mostly reacted on posts of various discussants (not just on one of the discussants) making online discussion similar to regular conversation. After elimnating repeated posts, the number of discussants decreased to 365.

Among the discussants, we observed four persons who, based on the erudition of the post, did not have any knowledge in topic discussed to be able to judge it objectively. Based on the evaluation of their posts, we may classify them as the politician's opponents. Their posts contained arguments which were of the most complex nature. It is interesting that at least in two cases they proposed solutions that were similar to solutions of the author of the project, nevertheless, these were not stated in the shared article and status. They did it based on their experience in Austria[91] or their personal experience with integrated children.[92] Supporters of the status were in their statements much more concise and they did not argue or seek solutions. The politician's status was shared on Facebook 664 times and it became the source of other discussions that, however, we do not analyze in this contribution due to spatial restrictions.

---

91 Comment on Boris Kollár's Facebook page, May 15, 2016 (10:51 p.m.)–May
    16, 2016 (10:02 a.m.), accessed January 25, 2017, https://www.facebook.com/
    permalink.php?story_fbid=1614954265492309&id=1464024763918594.
92 Comment on Boris Kollár's Facebook page, May 14, 2016 (11:19 p.m.), accessed
    January 25, 2017, https://www.facebook.com/permalink.php?story_fbid=1614
    954265492309&id=1464024763918594.

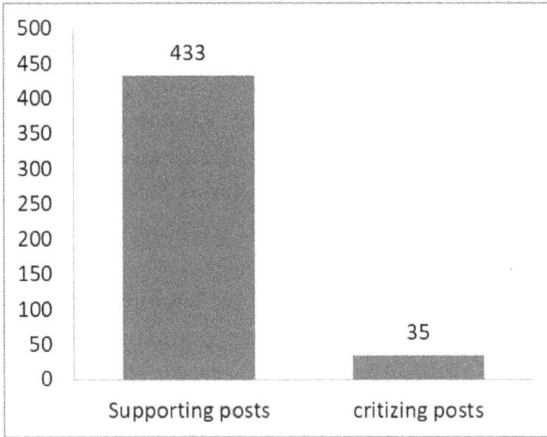

Image 8: The number of supportive and critical posts in the debate on the politician's status on Facebook confirms that the Internet does not yet serve to discuss but support attitudes.

2.8 Summary

The role of media is not to solve the integration of minorities but by following ethical norms to seek and offer the public the possibility to think about it. Media may either support integration processes or prevent them, especially in a way of grasping the topic regarding minorities either by informing about integration or by creating stereotypes and negative images about *"the others"*. Speaking of integration, the positive depiction of topics by media is not necessary, but the fair handling of topics concerning minorities is.

Although the results of our research could not be generalized, they partially confirm assumptions about correlation and gradation of the prejudices and stereotypes presented by media on the Internet statuses of politicians and their supporters.

Despite the dominance of statements supporting the politician's stereotypical opinion we also found posts that relativize negative attitudes of critics of the Internet as a means for social discussion by their opposite attitude and discussion. Although majority of people discussing supported each other and agreed with the opponents of the status, his supporters argued little and did not attack each other. At the same time, we found practical proposals to solve the problem in the discussion. It is questionable as to what extent the opposite opinions and proposals of the people discussing may change the opinion of the author of the status. Based on the recent performance of Boris Kollár in a discussion program of social service broadcasting Radio and Television of Slovakia called O 5 minút 12 (12 in 5 Minutes) of 15 January, 2017,[93] we assume that stereotypical opinions persist.

Results of our analysis do not doubt professionalism of all journalists. The latest research of the Romano Kher Company states the growth of posts *"in which the authors attempt to overcome stereotypes."*[94] Results of the research, however, confirm the assumption that there are media on the Internet deforming the reality, yet they look for negatives in the proposals for solutions of problems; they do not analyze and use aggressive style.

It would not pose a problem if they were not promoted by individuals seen as elites by the public. In our case, it was a deputy of the National Council of the Slovak Republic. We believe that potential removal of Internet statuses that contain prejudices and stereotypes in cases when an author explicitly does not attack a particular person does not solve the issue.

Only education in the sphere of media literacy and human-led social sciences may contribute to the ability of the public to perceive media content and politicians' opinions critically. Important positions in regard to informing about the possibilities of social integration still belong to media, professionals and elites.

---

93 „O 5 minút 12."
94 Newton media, *Mediálna analýza pre Romano Kher – Rómsky dom: 1. júl–31. október 2016*, 15.

3 Current Issues of Public Media

The position of the European public media is historically based on a concept of the British BBC from where public broadcasting was gradually spread also to some non-European and overseas countries (e.g. Canada) during the 20th century[95]. However, according to McQuail, a uniform and generally accepted theory of public broadcasting has never existed and systems of public broadcasting differ in separate countries.[96] In their publication *Media Systems in Postmodern World*, Hallin and Mancini compared media systems operating in 18 countries, and although they were able to define certain common elements of separate systems and create three models of media, they admitted that the model does not work in any of the researched states in *"ideal form"*.[97] According to McQuail, it is at least possible to determine common targets which should be fulfilled by public media according to national legislation. These are the following:

- full-area signal coverage;
- service to all relevant opinions, attitudes and interests;
- service for minorities;
- service for political parties;
- support for national culture;
- provision for impartial and balanced information, including controversial topics;
- preferring of public interest before financial one;
- provision of information of high "quality", whereby quality is defined differently.[98]

It is important to mention in this connection the Council of Europe, an institution within the European region, which takes care of freedom of information distribution and the right of access to relevant, impartial and objective information for a long time. It often expresses issues of public

---

95 Jirák and Köpplová, Masová média, 162.
96 McQuail, Úvod do teorie masové komunikace, 191.
97 Hallin and Mancini, Systémy médií v postmoderním světe, 40.
98 McQuail, Úvod do teorie masové komunikace, 192.

broadcasting and defines minimum requirements related to its operation, which should be reflected upon the national legislation of each state.

Within its media policy, the European Union also deals with the terms such as *"public service media"*, broadcasting in *"public interest"* etc.; however, it justifies its support to this form of broadcasting differently than it is understood by the Council of Europe. The European Union stresses a need for free information exchange and declares a need to eliminate all obstacles in television and radio broadcasting between states; however, representatives of the European Union believe that it can be achieved by supporting competition in the media market.[99] Overall, the European Union approaches the issue of media particularly from an economic perspective. On one side, it declares that media as business enterprises do not have the same rules as are applied in other spheres of businesses and that states are entitled, or better to say obliged, to regulating the broadcasting, but on the other hand, the European Union emphasizes that media are important players on the labor market and within the economic exchange of information.

However, the European Union does not question the importance to promote a dual form of broadcasting as a traditional media system in the European region. Public service broadcasting as a part of democratic establishment and a tool for ensuring the right to information and to a cultural heritage is declared by the Amsterdam Treaty of 1999 in a special section (Protocol on the System of Public Broadcasting in the Member States). It is also emphasized here that the Member States have a right to fund the public service broadcasting to the extent which does not significantly affect economic competition and business conditions within the Union.[100] Identical wording of this Protocol is a part of the Treaty on Functioning of the European Union.[101] It can be stated here that despite the European Union emphasizing a need for public service broadcasters as public information intermediators and distributors of the European cultural heritage in public interest, it also considers the role of media as an important player in the

---

99   European Union, Directive in Audio-Visual Media Services, codified wording, online.

100 European Union, Amsterdam Treaty, online.

101 European Union, Treaty on Functioning of the European Union, online.

COUNCIL OF EUROPE

CONSEIL DE L'EUROPE

Image 9: Logo of Council of Europe (Source: Council of Europe, 2017, https://www.coe.int/documents/16695/994584/COE-Logo-Quadri.png/ ee7b1fc6-055b-490b-a59b-a65969e440a2?t=1371222819000)

economic market (regardless of their content or a target of their spreading), and so information is understood as goods.

3.1 Activity of the Council of Europe in the Field of Public Broadcasting

A key Convention on Cross-Border Television defining basic principles which should be observed and enforced by each democratic state was signed in 1989 in Strasbourg at the Council of Europe. This Convention deals with issues of freedom of expression and transmission of information; liability of a transmitter for information it broadcasts and obligation of a transmitter to process such information professionally, with a right of the public to access information and important cultural, political and other social events; and plurality of information, with rules for screening of European works and issues of determination of advertising times and other forms of commercial media communication. This Convention also defines the right of a person directly affected by a content of broadcasting to adequate remedial measure that enables a such person to react on published information related to them adequately and on time (so-called right to answer).[102]

The Council of Europe defined its media policy in the field of public service broadcasting in 2007 in its Recommendation CM/Rec (2007) 3 of the Committee of Ministers of the Member States about the task of public service media (PSM) in information society, where it started to use the term *"public service media"* or PSM for the first time instead of the

---

102 Council of Europe, Convention on Cross-Border Television, online.

original term *"public service broadcasting"*, abbreviated as PSB. In contrast to the term "broadcasting", the term *"public service media"* is technologically neutral as a reaction of the Council of Europe to new procedures in the field of spreading of information.[103] At the same time, the Council of Europe emphasizes that due to the fact that mainly the young generation still more often diverts from traditional media and prefers new media and social networks, it is important that PSM respond to this development and search for modern forms of information spreading. Here, operating PSM are understood as an inevitable assumption of democratic discussion and as a tool for the spreading of different thoughts and opinions, plurality of information and cultural diversity. States are obliged to ensure both a legislative frame for proper operation of PSM and sufficient funds, so the mission of PSM will not be only at the declared level, but will be reflected in their day-to-day activities.[104]

In this connection, the Council of Europe recommends the Member States to:

– define roles and activities of PSM in the media market;
– provide media with sufficient technical background that reflects technological changes in the field of spreading of information and changes in information needs and expectations of audience in the digital era. The Council of Europe emphasizes that the PSM should also provide services which are more increasingly promoted on the market, e.g. personalized interactive content or broadcasting on-demand.
– modify new forms of communication legislatively so all ways of communication with public offered by these new media could be used, particularly to support wider democratic, social and cultural participation of public on public communication. These are media of public service, which should primarily support effective and proper control of government and international clusters and strengthen democratic principles;

---

103 Jakubowicz, "A New Promise for Public Service Provision in the Information Society," 193–227.
104 Council of Europe, Recommendation CM/Rec(2007)3 of the Committee of Ministers to Member States on the remit of public service media in the information society, online.

- to enable PSM to respond to new challenges of the information society, properly and effectively taking into account the existing European dual media system and rules of the media market and market competition;
- to enable all inhabitants, social groups, minorities, disadvantaged citizens etc. access to media services by several information channels. However, a principle of universality does not apply only to groups of inhabitants, but also to content and technical aspects of media;
- to provide financial and organizational support so the above-mentioned commitments of PSM could be executed while maintaining the editorial freedom and autonomy of PSM within the existing media system.

In contrast to private media enterprises, PSM should offer value-added programs – it means programs which respect and fulfil the public interest in addition to their other functions (information, cultural, educational and entertaining).[105]

The Council of Europe points out that the task of PSM is mainly to bring information about members of other cultures and religions with the help of new digital technologies in such a way that they support international dialog in this era of globalization and migration . It is an obligation of media to help prevent conflicts in the society and create an atmosphere of tolerance by broadcasting impartial and objective news. However, it can be ensured only in the case that PSM will be trusted by its audience and will be considered as reliable, professional and of a high ethical standard.[106]

3.2 Public Service Broadcasting in Slovakia

In the Slovak territory, the first PSB was established later in 1991 when the then legislative authority – the Slovak National Council – adopted Act No. 254/1991 Coll. on Slovak television and Act No. 255/1991 Coll. on Slovak radio. Both institutions were defined as *"national, independent, public service, informative, cultural and educational"* and their role was to *"serve the public"*. Both Slovak radio and Slovak television were financially supported directly from the state budget similarly as contributory

---

105 Ibid., online.
106 Ibid., online.

Image 10: In the middle of the picture, there is the building of Slovakia Radio in Bratislava (Author of photo: Andrej Bohuš, private archive, 2016)

organizations and they were allocated an independent budget category.[107] Television and radio had rather a status of state television towards the state whereas financial provision was completely in the hands of the government. Activity of both media should have been based on principles of independence and professionalism; however, the actual preserving of independence of political power was questionable in regard to the way of the creating of their bodies and the already-mentioned way of financing back then. Independence and impartiality of media should have been provided by the council, whose members were appointed by the Presidency of the Slovak National Council, the government of the Slovak Republic and the head of the broadcaster. Only a smaller part of the members of the Council

---

107 NR SR, *Zákon č. 254/1991 Zb. o Slovenskej televízii a zákon č. 255/1991 Zb. o Slovenskom rozhlase*, online.

Image 11: The building of RTVS, Slovak public broadcaster (Author of photo: Miroslava Dobrotková, private archive)

was appointed by so-called consulting committee, which was an authority composed of representatives of political parties that were not active in the parliament, representatives of the church and representatives of the civil society. This authority had only an advisory role. The Central director was a statutory authority appointed also by the Presidency of the Slovak National Council, so there was a connection of management of PSM to the government and parliamentary leadership and also a mutual intercon-nection between the statutory authority of media and the authority that was supposed to provide independence and impartiality of the content of broadcasting. This system of control of PSM was changed in October, 1992.[108] Members of the Council of the Slovak television and the Council of the Slovak radio as well as central directors were appointed by the National Council of the Slovak Republic since then. In autumn 1991, The Federal Council for Radio and Television Broadcasting was established and its role was to promote interests of the public in broadcasting (so it was some predecessor of the current Council for Broadcasting and Retransmission); however, the Federal Council was not authorized to sanction media established by the Act of the Slovak National Council, that means neither the Slovak television nor the Slovak radio. It was only an advisory authority towards them.[109]

3.3 On the Terms of Public Service and Public Interest

Broadcasting of PSM is understood as a public service and their obligation is to spread mainly information in public interest. The term public interest is not clearly defined; however, the content of this term is specified in various documents on international level. In general, it is the interest in gaining information useful for an individual and communities in society and information needed for socially excluded and disadvantaged groups of population from impartial news, commentaries and opinions.[110]

Spheres or questions that belong among information in public interest have been defined by the European Court of Human Rights through its decisions for several decades when it deals with cases of breaching the rights mainly pursuant to articles 8 (Right to a private and family life), 9 (Freedom of thought, conscience and religion) and 10 (Freedom of thought, conscience and religion).[111]

---

108 NR, SR, *Zákon č. 482/1992 Zb., ktorým sa mení a dopĺňa zákon Slovenskej národnej rady č. 254/1991 Zb. o Slovenskej televízii a zákon č. 483/1992 Zb. ktorým sa mení a dopĺňa zákon Slovenskej národnej rady č. 255/1991 Zb. o Slovenskom rozhlase*, online.
109 Ibid., online.
110 Council of Europe, Recommendation CM/Rec(2007)3 of the Committee of Ministers to Member States on the remit of public service media in the information society, online.
111 Rada Európy, Dohovor o ochrane ľudských práv a základných slobôd, online.

Information that belong to public interest are:

- regarding public functionary and performing of public function not necessarily in the sphere of politics (e.g. decision of Alfantakis against Greece, 2010);
- about handling of public property (decision of Marônek against Slovakia, 2001);
- about investigation of criminal offenses in all stages of criminal proceedings (Standard Verlags GmbH against Austria, 2012);
- about problems of minorities, cultural diversity (e.g. decision of Aksu against Turkey, 2010).[112]

In Slovak Administrative Code, the terms public service and public interest are, however, defined differently, but their nature remains the same. The sphere of programs that meet the requirement of the program in public interest is stipulated by Act No. 532/2010 Coll. about Radio and Television of Slovakia (RTVS) as well as Act No. 308/2000 Coll on broadcasting and retransmission. Under § 3 sec. 2 Act on RTVS, public service in the sphere of broadcasting means spreading of such program service that is *universal from the aspect of geographical impact, program diversified, prepared on the principle of editorial independence through qualified labor force and with the sense for social responsibility and which develops cultural level of listeners and viewers and provides space for current cultural and artistic activities, mediates space for current cultural and artistic activities, mediates cultural values of other nations and is financed especially from public resources.*[113] Programs of public service should be based on principles of democracy and humanism, should refuse any discrimination, support cultural awareness of population, responsibility towards the environment and lead recipients to creating opinions based on verified facts.[114]

---

112 Voorhoof et al., Freedom of Expression, the Media and Journalists: Case-law of the European Court of Human Right, online.
113 NR SR, *Zákon č. 532/2010 Z.z. o Rozhlase a televízii Slovenska a o zmene a doplnení niektorých zákonov*, §3 ods. 2.
114 NR SR, *Zákon č. 532/2010 Z.z. o Rozhlase a televízii Slovenska a o zmene a doplnení niektorých zákonov*, § 3 ods. 3.

The current draft amendment on RTVS, which is in an interdepartmental comment procedure, defines a new obligation of RTVS – to secure continuous broadcasting of program service through website domain RTVS and electronic application of RTVS in real time.[115] Legislator relatively tardily reacts on situations when technology enables such a form of broadcasting almost to every owner of mobile device. It is not possible to say yet if the amendment will be passed in the future. From the aspect of implementing these requirements into practice, several problems occur. Securing broadcasting in the entire territory, especially in the great majority of Slovakia, and providing space for cultural and artistic program within broadcasting is possible relatively easily; however, for the actual implementation of professionalism, expertness and responsibility in work of a journalist, no public institution has a role. The Council for Broadcasting and Retransmission, press councils or other public and self-governing regulatory bodies have authorization to point out failures of representatives of media in these spheres and to judge these failures in a certain way, respectively to sanction them; however, these requirements may be met with only in a case if a producer or a journalist is internally convinced about their rightness and decides to implement them into their work. According to Remišová, for a proper job performance of a journalist, professional journalistic theoretical education, broader social general knowledge, quality language preparation and character including primarily fairness, courageousness, responsibility, the ability of empathy, self-reflection and courage are necessary.[116]

We would also add to the mentioned enumeration of characteristics an effort to educate oneself constantly and certain stress resistance against pressure inside a media institution. These are undoubtedly characteristics that cannot be required from a graduate even though they may have a very high quality education, general knowledge of politics, economics and other disciplines and knowledge of theoretical principles of one's future profession. It is not possible to learn fairness, responsibility or professional approach, it is necessary to achieve them. It is right that a requirement for qualification, responsibility and professionalism is rooted in the law

---

115 Informatívne konsolidované znenie právneho predpisu 532/2010 Z.z.
116 Remišová, Etika médií, 166.

because it partially strengthens the status of an independent journalist within a media structure; however, without the existence of effective control mechanism that would guarantee this independence and other rights of journalists and would function independently from media management, the requirements remains only on a declaratory level.

Editorial independence of internal and external coworkers of RTVS is defined within internal rules of RTVS. The Statute of Program Workers and Coworkers of RTVS that RTVS is obliged to adopt (§ 4 sec. 2 Act No. 532/2010 Coll.) on RTVS defines the status of workers of RTVS within the structure of RTVS but externally against third parties and defines unacceptable conduct of a worker. The statute applies to any and all persons that participate in program production and is naturally binding for both parties, not only for RTVS. The statute especially adjudges a producer of a program to inform in advance that they cannot elaborate a certain topic and their superior is obliged to release them from the preparation of a given task without any penalties. Workers' reasons may be both objective and subjective; it basically means any reason. Workers may refuse to perform a task, for instance, due to topic controversy or due to the fact that they disagree with an instruction on how to elaborate a topic. On the other hand, RTVS shall respect the freedom of speech of its coworkers and support opinion plurality.[117] Although we are still in the sphere of broadcasting of a public service, these guarantees do not allow workers of RTVS to spread anything regardless of consequences but to use these rights in favor of providing impartial, true and professionally prepared information. Intentional spreading of unfounded information is unacceptable; however, it does not mean that a worker of RTVS is not authorized to inform about the existence of discussion on topics considered to be controversial or conspiratorial, although they should inform about the fact that these topics are not founded (yet) or there are many contradictory opinions on them.

Activities of the workers of RTVS in a political grouping, interest association or opinion association as well as entrepreneurship is basically allowed; however, a worker cannot connect these activities to their work for RTVS or they cannot present their political, religious or other interest

---

117 „Štatút programových pracovníkov a spolupracovníkov RTVS."

opinions in a way as if they were opinions of RTVS. Acting in advertisement is absolutely inadmissible. Both parties shall respect these rules under any circumstances to make them work effectively. In a well-known affair of a presenter of RTVS, Natália Žembová, the presenter in a commercial spot for Alliance for Family, should have been aware of the fact that she breached internal regulations of her employer in a serious way (not taking her conviction into consideration) and also she had to be aware of her possible dismissal from work. It was not a spot content itself but the fact that it was a spot that may be considered to be a political commercial because regarding the current political fight (campaign prior to voting in referendum) it presented and supported a certain opinion.

Under the act on broadcasting and retransmission, a program in public interest is defined as a program that *"focuses on satisfying information and cultural needs of listeners or viewers in the entire area covered by a broadcaster with its signal"*, such as:

1. program for juveniles focused on educational and information purpose;
2. news service;
3. program aimed at education and training, science and research;
4. program providing legal and other information; supporting healthy lifestyle; providing information on nature, conservation and protection of the environment and protection of life, health and property and road safety;
5. program presenting culture with an emphasis on Slovak national culture and culture of national minorities and ethnic groups, their life and opinions;
6. program presenting a religious activity;
7. program aimed at groups of persons in unfavorable social situations.[118]

Entertainment programs, if they meet some of the aforementioned objectives, may be classified as programs in public interest.

It is possible to generalize that information in public interest is such information that is necessary for human existence in society and for performing their social, cultural and economic needs. The content of the term public

---

118 NR SR, *Zákon č. 308/2000 Z.z. o vysielaní a retransmisii*, online.

interest is relatively clearly defined; however, the sphere of topic and media outputs belonging to this term is naturally not closed.

The question who gave some of the aforementioned institutions or legislators permission to define what public interest is is legitimate yet wrongly asked; it is a misunderstanding of the problem because regarding public interest, the crucial is what is important or needed for majority of society members and not what an individual subjectively considers to be important and needs for themselves regardless of others.

3.4 Viewership of Public Service Media

Although the European Convention on Transfrontier Television deals with broadcasting as such regardless of the status of broadcasters in the media market, its principles binding for contracting states should be implemented especially in PSB. It is an obligation to spread programs that necessarily secure a television deciding position on the media market; however, they provide the public with quality information from politics, culture, education, health care etc., they follow European cultural heritage and develop European audiovisual production. Public service broadcasting cannot be assessed only from the aspect of its commercial success, financial returns of program or their viewership because the fundamental reason of the existence of PSM is providing access to information to the widest range of recipients. Public service broadcasting shall provide viewers with such information the spreading of which is not interesting for commercial media and therefore it contributes to plurality of information. An argument for restricting of PSB or restricting of its financing is also not an interest of majority of the audience in a given sphere of information because the value of information and opinions for the life of an individual is not determined by the fact how many people are interested in the information or opinion.

McQuail considers the trend of decreasing of their viewership as one of the crucial problems of public media nowadays.[119] We do not notice this trend in the Slovak Republic. Based on the results of the research on media viewership that is conducted by Median SK agency with the complex research on consumption, media and lifestyle, it is obvious that viewership

---

119 McQuail, Úvod do teorie masové komunikace, 192–193.

of circuits of RTVS does not decrease even if it slightly increases in case of television circuits of Jednotka. During 2011–2016 (in 2016 the subject of a research was viewership for the first 3 quarters of the year), the viewership of Jednotka increased from 17% to 25% and viewership of RTVS was around 16% –18%.[120] The trend of increasing of the viewership of the television is eventually confirmed by an annual report on RTVS in 2015; however, this is focused on the share of the television on the market. It simultaneously confirms a slight increase of viewership of the young audience.[121]

When we look at the numbers of viewers and listeners of the medzi of public service in Slovakia mentioned above in calculating the media market share, we can see that the trend of increasing the number of viewership is confirmed. We can see it in the following graph showing the trends of viewership from 2011 till 2016 (Rádio Slovensko and Rádio Regina are the radio stations of RTVS and Jednotka is a television station of RTVS):

Certain disinterest in questions of public interest, ignorance and the inability to give information on the European Union context has been informing about what on a long-term basis may be considered problematic. Robert W. McChesney sees the reasons of this condition in the so-called professionalism of journalism. Journalists who try to present themselves as independent and impartial rely on official sources of news, it means on politicians and other representatives of public administration; they publish official announcements and reactions of the other party; however, they do not comment, do not put them into context and in case of contradictory information they do not find out what party gave a false statement. Although media avoid accusations of being biased in favor of some opinion, they also support depoliticization and discourage the public from engaging in political discussions and civic engagement.[122] The author even claims that to assign to media nowadays their traditional role – watchdog of democracy – is illusory because media serve the middle and higher classes due

---

120 MEDIAN SK, *MML – TGI, národný prieskum spotreby, médií, a životného štýlu, Market & Media & Lifestyle – TGI*, online.
121 RTVS, Výročná správa o činnosti Rozhlasu a televízie Slovenska za rok 2015, 1–127.
122 McChesney, Problém médií. Jak uvažovat o dnešních médiích, 14–19.

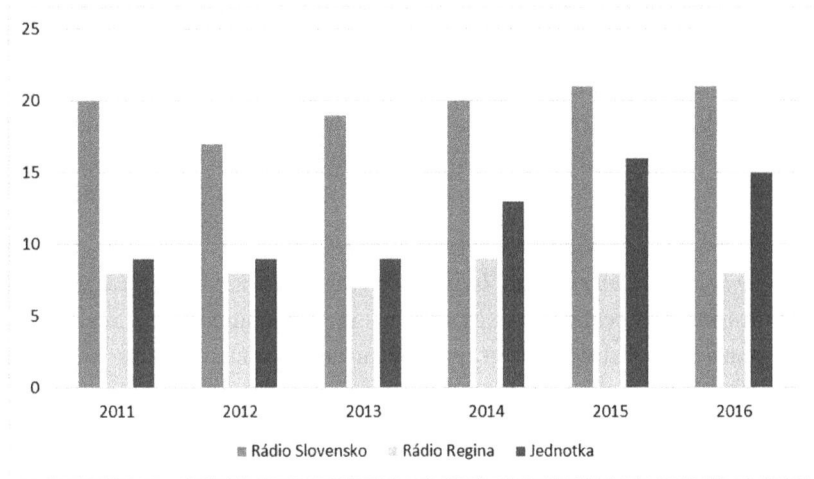

Image 12: Source: MEDIAN SK, MML – TGI, národný prieskum spotreby, médií, a životného štýlu, Market & Media & Lifestyle – TGI, 2011, 2012, 2013, 2014, 2015 and 2016, online.

to the fact that they mainly focus on potential and lucrative consumers.[123] Commercialization of media and orientation on audience in active age (in other words, on potential consumers that have their own income) may not be basically denied; however, in the context of slight increase of viewership of PSM in recent years, it may be stated that it is a quite pessimistic opinion.

3.5 Funding of Public Service Media

Editorial independence and financing of PSM (mostly) from public funds belong to basic assumptions for securing interest of public in objective and verified information. There is a model of financing PSM from purpose contribution paid by the public in Europe. Obligation to pay this contribution is, for instance, related to ownership of television and radio receiver or other technological device capable of capturing and recording of PSB

---

123 Ibid., 37.

(Great Britain[124], Czech Republic[125], Austria[126]) for energy consumption (Slovakia[127]).

Due to the existence of responsibility of media for funds provided by the public budget, there are requirements that are naturally argumentative.[128]

Total revenue of RTVS under Act No. 532/2010 Coll. on RTVS consists of following items:

- *remittance on public services (end-user charges);*
- *contribution from the state budget provided under the contract with the state* aimed for realization of programs in public interest, for realization of purpose investment projects or remittance of costs for providing of broadcasting abroad (in case of radio broadcasting);
- revenue from broadcasting of media commercial communication (definition of media commercial communication is included in Act No. 308/2000 Coll. on broadcasting and retransmission[129]. This term is broader than the term advertising; advertising is only one of the forms of media commercial communication);
- *Sponsorship* used for direct or indirect financing of programs. It is again one of the forms of media commercial communication and therefore it is a redundant provision;
- revenue from rent and sale of property of *RTVS;*
- *revenues from bank deposits* and from financial investments, with the exception of revenues of deposits of financial funds provided to RTVS by the state under the contract; these revenues mean revenues of the state budget;
- *donations* from natural persons and legal entities that cannot fall under the term sponsorship;

---

124 "Do you need a TV licence?"
125 PSP ČR, *Zákon č. 348/2005 Sb. o rozhlasových a televizních poplatcích a o změně některých zákonů,* online.
126 „Gebühren Info Service".
127 NR SR, *Zákon č. 340/2012 Z.z. o úhrade za služby verejnosti poskytované Rozhlasom a televíziou Slovenska a o zmene a doplnení niektorých zákonov,* online.
128 McQuail, Úvod do teorie masové komunikace, 192.
129 NR SR, *Zákon č. 308/2000 Z.z. o vysielaní a retransmisii,* online.

- *heritage* in favor of RTVS;
- *grants* from natural persons and legal entities for performing tasks in public interest that are not under program sponsorship;
- other revenues.

3.6 User Charges

RTVS is primarily financed from contribution from the so-called remittance for public services provided by RTVS; however, this amount of remittance is approx. 50% (in 2015)[130] and 59% (in 2014) from the total income of RTVS[131]. The range of payers, the amount of remittance and other conditions is amended by Act No. 340/2012 Coll. on remittance for services provided by RTVS. As it is stated in a reasoning report of the Act, during the Act preparation there were also considerations about funding of RTVS mostly from the state budget, however, with the aim to provide media independence and strengthen direct relationship with partial support by the state. Non-binding of charge obligation for electricity consumption was adopted because a legislator believed in more effective collection of charges.[132] The legislator probably thought that the database of electricity consumers is more exact and basically complete compared to the database of device owners for perception of television or radio signal. The authorized access for the remittance collector into the customer database of the electricity supplier and identification of possible non-payers is allowed by § 9 sec.2 letter a) Act that defines the obligation of suppliers to inform RTVS as a collector about the list of consumers.

Based on a still valid charge of end-user charges of RTVS, it is not able to cover all costs solely from these revenues. That is also one of the reasons why the state tries to enforce a higher amount of end-user charges. The

---

130 RTVS, Výročná správa o činnosti Rozhlasu a televízie Slovenska za rok 2015, 1–127.
131 RTVS, Výročná správa o činnosti Rozhlasu a televízie Slovenska za rok 2014, 1–193.
132 „Dôvodová správa k Zákonu č. 340/2012 Z.z. o úhrade za služby verejnosti poskytované Rozhlasom a televíziou Slovenska a o zmene a doplnení niektorých zákonov."

amendment act on remittance for public service fundamentally amended the obligation to pay end-user charges not only from the aspect of the amount of charge but also from the aspect of the ways of its determination and determination of the range of obligatory persons. The sum of the charge is set by the act what means that for its increase amendment of law and therefore voting in the parliament is required. The rate of charge will be determined by the ministry of culture by generally binding legal regulation; the amendment does not have be necessarily passed by the National Council of the Slovak Republic. The ministry will be partially limited by the fact that a new rate of the charge may range depending on limits set by a committee, a new advisory authority of the ministry in the sector of funding of PSB. Committee members, however, will be appointed by the minister, so their independence from the ministry cannot be expected, though these will be experts in the field of broadcasting and audiovisual production.[133] The meaning of the existence of the committee is to analyze the financial situation of RTVS, which is, however, prepared by RTVS itself within its annual reports and the "approval" of the minister's decision on further increasing of end-user charges. On one hand, we agree with the fact that the amount of end-user charges is needed to be amended on a regular basis; however, this process may be legislatively amended so it will not be dependent on the decision of one person (the minister), e.g., it would be possible to connect the determination of the rate of end-user charges to the development of an average salary or development of inflation.

3.7 Funding from the State Budget

Contract with the state on providing funds to secure PSB is entered always for the period of 5 years; however, the contract text itself has the character of a framework contract, i.e., it contains only general announcement about the obligation of RTVS to conduct programs in public interest that are considered to be an original television and radio program production and on the other hand commitment of the state to financially contribute to this activity.[134] Although another commitment of RTVS, which is performing

---

133 Informatívne konsolidované znenie právneho predpisu 340/2012 Z.z.
134 NR SR, *Zákon č. 532/2010 Z.z. o Rozhlase a televízii Slovenska*, online.

of investment projects related to the activity of RTVS, is only declared, so basically it does not exist unless clearly defined in contract amendment. The current contract with the state is concluded for the period from 2013 to 2017, whereas the state is obliged to financially contribute to the operation of RTVS by the sum of at least 15.000.000 euros annually.[135]

The actual sum provided by the state in a given year is determined by several amendments to the contract where genre, running time and programs that are supposed to be produced using these funds are more clearly defined. The content of amendment is a result of negotiation of the ministry of culture and representatives of RTVS. Amendment system to framework contract is relatively inflexible and non-transparent. Although the public may look these amendments up relatively easily through the website domains of RTVS and the ministry of culture, the selection process of programs that will be funded by the state budget and reason for their choice of programs either not communicated publicly or only general reason are stated, meeting some of the objectives of PSB. Financial support from the state budget itself does not mean a problem (financial support of public service is an obligation of the state); the problem is shortage of information provided to the public regarding the process of this funding.

Although there is an act amendment on RTVS and in the second half of the years together with the amendment act on public service in interdepartmental comments, legislation of the contract with the state practically remains unchanged (according to the current wording of the amendment).[136]

3.8 Future of Slovak Media of Public Service

If plurality of information and relatively easy approach of the public to impartial, verified and objective information that meet the requirement for information in public interest should be secured, then the existence of PSB is necessary. Although the independence of the media of public service from representatives of political power is the fundamental requirement, it does mean that the state has nothing in common with broadcasting. It is

---

135 „Zmluva o zabezpečení služieb verejnosti v oblasti rozhlasového a televízneho vysielania 2013–2017."
136 Informatívne konsolidované znenie právneho predpisu 532/2010 Z.z.

the obligation of the state to legislatively secure the status of PSB within the media market and the status of producers of this broadcasting so they can perform their duties freely and independently and guarantee funding of this broadcasting to such an extent that the message of the media of public service will not only be declared in legal regulations but in fact implemented into broadcasting. At the same time, the obligation of the state is constantly to explain to the public why the PSB is important and why the discussion of this topic should not be limited only to the obligation of signal receivers to pay for broadcasting, because the question is not if public service is meaningful but rather what it should be like.

Within the organizational structure of a public service broadcaster, we find it necessary to create a control mechanism that provides presenters with support in case of realization of their right to refuse the instruction of their superior to elaborate information in a certain way. Presenters are in a labor relation with the medium and always in a subordinate position and it is not possible nowadays to legitimately expect them to make a decision between an obligation to elaborate a certain information impartially and objectively on one hand and on the other hand remaining in their function that they will always decide for impartiality.

In the sphere of funding of PSB, it would be suitable to the system of negotiation on the content of the contract with the state more comprehensible to engage independent media professionals into program selection financially supported by the state. If broadcasting producers have an opportunity to approach broadcasting conceptually and effectively and plan the broadcasting, then it is necessary to change this system in a way that annual "amending" of the contract with the state will be removed and broadcasting content funded by the state budget will be made for several years in advance. Amendments would then discuss only individual, partial problems that would naturally occur during the preparation of more demanding programs.

Despite good viewership of RTVS in Slovakia, it is necessary to spread broadcasting in order to make it available also for recipients who do not want to watch broadcasting in a fixed time but anytime and for recipients who want to create their own broadcasting structure from a variety of programs offered. Nowadays, majority of households have access to high-speed Internet, and mobile electronic devices are on such technological level that they are able to transmit broadcasting in high quality, and both options are technically available. The role of a legislator is then to root broadcasting in public interest also through the website domain of RTVS and through mobile applications.

4 The Phenomenon of Alternative Media in Slovakia

Media were especially in their beginnings mediators of information of the ruling classes. Predecessors of media in China were in the form of secret messages aimed exclusively for the ruling dynasties. Certain indications of spreading information independent of the ruling class may be found already in the Middle Ages, yet their real boom occurred with the invention of letterpress and strengthening of capitalism. Since then we may find many cases when media began to serve for the expanding of other opinions. For instance, the first newspaper published in the territory of Slovakia, Mercurius veridicus ex Hungaria of 1705–1710, was printed in times of the anti-Habsburg uprising of Francis II Rákóczi[137] as "anti-propaganda" of the kuruc rebels against the emperor newspaper Wienerische Diarum. During the following centuries, it was common that journals were censored, fined, and eventually completely banned. In the territory of Slovakia this, situation persisted until 1989. However, it would be incorrect to identify the historical fight for freedom of the press with the production of alternative media. The aim is to point at the fact that attempts for another, different interpretation of events are present throughout the entire development of media until now.

In regard to the period of The Czechoslovak Socialist Republic, media aimed at Czechoslovakia that pointed out that opinion alternative with their content alongside samizdat periodicals should not be omitted, especially radio broadcasting of stations such as Slobodná Európa (Free Europe) and Hlas Ameriky (The Voice of America). Although on the other side of an imaginary wall of the Cold War where the freedom of speech and expression were rooted, media were active based on their belief that freedom in society, particularly in media, is not complete and sufficient (e.g. printed periodicals of the protest movement against the war in Vietnam in the United States). These media may be understood as direct predecessors of current alternative media.

---

137 Chmelár, Uhorská tlačová politika (so zreteľom na slovenské novinárstvo), 24.

More systematic effort to establish alternative media may be seen later at the turn of 2012–2013 when the program Mlčanie (Silence) on Viva radio[138], broadcasting of the radio Slobodný vysielač (Free Broadcaster),[139] as well as publishing of the monthly Zem a Vek (Earth and Age)[140] began. Nowadays alternative media represent a phenomenon which part of professional public, especially mainstream (in this case competitive), media take a very skeptical stand against. At the same time, alternative media enjoy their increasing popularity among one part of recipients, while the other have a critical attitude based on information provided by mainstream media. Professional public in Slovakia, except for rare exceptions, have not drawn their attention to alternative media yet. This type of media, however, during an extremely short period of time became a phenomenon that currently polarizes the society. The aim of this chapter, therefore, will be to introduce detailed and chronological development of alternative media in Slovakia in a broader context, to connect to the journalists who established them, to name positives and negatives of this type of media as well as referring to works by foreign theoreticians to state some formulations that would help to understand the phenomenon of Slovak alternative media and to outline their further development at the same time.

4.1 What Is the Alternative?

Determination of several definitions that would contribute to better understanding of alternative media may serve as the base for analysis of current situation of alternative media in Slovakia. At the beginning, it is necessary to say that professional public abroad could agree neither on unanimous definitions nor on unanimous naming so far. In regard to the media that cannot be classified as mainstream selected authors therefore use not only name *"alternative"* but expressions such as "independent"[141], "civil"[142],

---

138 „Archív."
139 „Mediálne.sk: Z Banskej Bystrice sa (opäť) ozve Slobodný vysielač."
140 „Zemavek.sk: Archív časopisov."
141 Rauch, "Exploring the Alternative – Mainstream dialectic," 125.
142 Rodriguez "Fissures in the mediascape: An international study of citizens media," in Rauch, "Exploring the alternative – mainstream dialectic: What "alternative media" means to a hybrid audience," 124–143.

"community"[143], "activist"[144], "dissident"[145] or "underground" (underground press)"[146] or "radical"[147] media.

This type of media is namely constituted as an opposition/alternative against something. The crucial criterion based on which they form a different opinion compared to the remaining part of media market is, however, determined by each media itself. Such criterion may be a financial independence from corporations or sponsors of advertising, independence from establishment, absence of editorial hierarchy, the amount of costs or territorial focus. Content is a specific criterion. In this case some authors find alternative media specializing in minorities in regard to their content – sexual, religious, language etc. Another frequent case represents alternative as an opinion opposition i.e. bringing news information as mainstream what may be understood either as new topics absent in mainstream or other opinions on topics and events presented in mainstream.

The definition of the British Royal Commission on the Press in material of 1977 belongs to the oldest available. Commission states three points characterizing alternative press:

1. Alternative publications dealing with opinions of minorities;
2. They express their attitude *"from hostile to generally spread opinions"*;
3. They identify themselves with opinions or they deal with topics that are not in the center of attention in publications standardly available in newsagent's shops.[148]

The greatness of media plays an import role according to Kranichová who claims that *"alternative"* is *"the aptest"* expression for designation of small and independent publishers because these publishers *"act as a counterweight to corporal media."*[149]

---

143 Downing, Radical media, 39.
144 Waltz, Alternative and activist media, 3–4.
145 "The propaganda system."
146 "Glossary."
147 Downing, Radical media, 5.
148 McGregor, Periodicals and the alternative press in Atton, Alternative media, 12.
149 Kranich, "A Question of Balance: The Role of Libraries in Providing Alternatives to the Mainstream Media," 85

Majority of authors, however, incline to the criterion of difference of published opinions. Hamilton claims that alternative media are important for *"clear expression of social order, different and often contradictory from the dominant one"*[150]. According to another definition, alternative media are even created as an open opposition against mainstream[151]. The founder of the magazine Counterpoise Charles Willett is of the opinion that alternative press *"expresses any ideal beyond what is correct, anything that is not accepted, not allowed, what is not available in corporate and governing mainstream."*[152]

In professional literature, we may find a term *"activist"* media. Waltz draws his attention to the fact that *"activist"* and *"alternative"* does not necessarily mean the same. As the name itself indicates, *"activist"* media encourage readers to be actively involved in social change. They may express any political conviction from extreme left to extreme right – in fact, the definition of a broad term *"activist"* should include media that support activities typical for mainstream as well such as voting for politicians by one's own choice or charity volunteering.[153]

Especially John Downing and Chris Atton focus on alternative media in their works on a long-term basis. Atton dedicated several publications to alternative media – for instance Alternative media[154], An alternative Internet[155] or Alternative journalism[156]. In An alternative Internet, the authors describes this part of media as *"the sequence of media projects, actions and networks that work against dominant, awaited (and broadly accepted) way "how to make" media or they try to develop their various forms."*[157]

---

150 Hamilton, "Alternative media: Conceptual difficulties, critical possibilities," 362.
151 Downmunt, Coyer, The Alternative media handbook, 1.
152 Willett, "The State of Alternative Publishing in America: Issues and Implications for Libraries," 14.
153 Waltz, Alternative and activist media, 3–4.
154 Atton, Alternative media, 172.
155 Atton, An alternative internet, 192.
156 Atton, Alternative journalism, 192.
157 Atton, Alternative internet, 9.

Downing has been dealing with the research of non-mainstream media from the first half of the 1980s. He is the author of the phrase *"radical media"*,[158] respectively "radical alternative media"[159] that is supposed to be more precise expression than *"alternative media."* The role of radical media is to express alternative vision against hegemonic policy, priorities and perspectives.[160] At the same time, Downing adds that speaking about alternative media is almost an oxymoron because *"everything in a certain moment is an alternative to something else."*[161]

Downmunt and Coyerová follow the mentioned statement to a certain degree – what defines media as an alternative in specific cultural and time period may be labeled as mainstream within a different place, time and culture[162]. For instance, Austrian television ORF (Österreichischer Rundfunk) was an alternative for residents of socialist Czechoslovakia before 1989 in regard to its broadcasting content – compared to Czechoslovak television stations that served as the local mainstream. In Austria itself, ORF was also a part of mainstream.

To characterize non-mainstream media using generally accepted definition is therefore demanding. For example, Abel doubts that there could be a meaningful definition for the phrase *"alternative media."*[163] Each alternative medium defines its *"alternativeness"* against mainstream itself by its focus or work organization. On the other hand, an attempt to understand alternative media through characteristics of what (mainstream) defines itself against would apparently bring no desirable effect. We therefore express our conviction that definition of alternative media depends on situation in a particular country or region in many aspects. Domestic social-political situation and its resulting information policy of mainstream determine the demand for absent information that is subsequently provided by the alternative.

---

158 Downing, Radical media: The political experience of alternative communication, 370.
159 Downing, Radical media: Rebelious communication and social movements, 426.
160 Downing, Radical media, 5.
161 Ibid., 9.
162 Downmunt, Coyer, The alternative media handbook, 1.
163 Abel, "An alternative press. Why?" in Atton, *Alternative media*, 9.

4.2 Beginnings of Current Alternative Media in Slovakia

The history of current alternative media in Slovakia is very short. As we mentioned at the beginning of this chapter, information alternative against regimes or their main media have always existed – e.g. resistance periodicals during the Second World War or samizdats in the period of socialism – although we would find only little examples of common attributes with the current alternative media. Similarly, in the time period after 1989, there are several media that were different from the main group in some aspects, but we cannot speak about alternative media in their current form. It is important that after-November development brought several events of worldwide importance where media (not only Slovak ones) were not successful in their role of independent and impartial provider of information. Slovak public very sensitively reacted mainly on the war in Yugoslavia in 1999 and also a war in Iraq in 2003. It is necessary to mention the color revolutions in republics of former USSR (especially in neighboring Ukraine), the series of revolutions and subsequent armed conflicts known as the Arab Spring; and from the domestic events, it was the Gorilla scandal that mobilized substantial part of the public at the tune of 2011 and 2012. Series of these protests was one of the biggest manifestations of dissatisfaction of society from November 1989. Especially in the period after parliamentary elections in 2012 – on the debris of protesting movement Gorilla, we may notice mobilization of marginal activist groups.

Right at the Gorilla protests which background is the center of attention of Tom Nicholson[164] and subsequently other smaller protest events after the election in 2012, an incentive for establishing alternative media may be found. In this environment, there is, for example, Slovak branch of a portal Idymedia[165]established and following attempt to establish the

---

164 Nicholson, Gorila, 191.
165 Independent Media Center- abbreviated as Indymedia was established in 1999 in the city of Seattle during multiple protests of anti-globalist movement. Indymedia functions on the principle of free contributions- i.e. anyone may publish his own articles or news on the website of local Inymedia. Editorial policy is selected by each local group according to their own belief. In general it includes removal or articles that according to editorial staff's opinion spread racism, sexism, demonstration of hatred and homophobia.

daily Verejnosť (The Public) that had a samizdat format.[166] At the beginning of the current alternative, there is especially the program Mlčanie (Silence) prepared and hosted by Tibor Rostas (former employee of TV Markíza[167]) on the Viva radio. It broadcasts from 2006 (on frequencies after the Twist radio),[168] and in the time period including Mlčanie (Silence) to the broadcasting in July 2012, it was with approximately 4% share on the market – the seventh most listened station in Slovakia and even the third in the Bratislava region[169]. Mlčanie (Silence) had a format of two-minute program broadcasted on every working day at 6:40 p.m.[170] Rostas who was also involved in the Gorilla protests, and especially in the later protests,[171] alternately dealt with political, economic or historic topics in the program – although he did not avoid the current situation. In 2012, he published a book of short essays based on individual episodes of the program. The title of the book is Mlčanie [Silence],[172] and in 2013 it belonged to TOP 10 bestsellers in Panta Rhei bookstores.[173] The same year Rostas published the second volume of Mlčanie,[174] and he started with publishing printed monthly named Zem a Vek [Earth and Age] with the subtitle *Hidden Information Without Censorship*.[175]

Zem a Vek taking alternative media into account had a quality graphic format from its beginning. According to the data of the editorial staff, five people participated in the content of 120-page magazine and the editorial staff attempted to assert themselves[176] on the market competing with mainstream periodicals with five thousand printouts.

---

166 The daily Verejnosť (The Public) was published in 2013–2014 in black and white format on one page of A4 size and could be easily copied.

167 „Vrtí pes chvostom alebo chvost psom?"

168 „Sme.sk: Rádio Viva má reláciu, v ktorej sa hovorí o tajomných skupinkách ovládajúcich svet."

169 „Radia.sk: počúvanosť 2+3 vlna 2012."

170 „Relácia Mlčanie – 001. Mlčanie."

171 „Lesk a bieda kurtizán konšpiračného mainstreamu."

172 „Pantarhei.sk: Eseje, úvahy, štúdie – Mlčanie."

173 „Sme.sk: Rádio Viva má reláciu, v ktorej sa hovorí o tajomných skupinkách ovládajúcich svet."

174 „Pantarhei.sk: Eseje, úvahy, štúdie – Mlčanie II."

175 „Zemavek.sk: Archív časopisov."

176 „tyzden.sk: Planéta Rostas."

The turn of 2012 and 2013 is simultaneously a period when preparations for the establishment of Internet radio of Slobodný vysielač began. Norbert Lichtner and two former redactors of Catholic radio Lumen Boris Koróni and Peter Kršiak were responsible for its launching. According to their own words, they wanted to substitute the role of PSM and provide some space for other topics that cannot be found in mainstream media and that are tabooed or censored[177].

At the same time, many Internet portals are active – their classification into alternative media is, however, questionable from many aspects. Some of them are openly linked to marginal political parties or associations (their motivation to social changes is therefore connected to an effort to achieve political influence) and others such as Hlavné správy [Main News] greatly use agency service of the TAST newswire.

The year 2013 was crucial from the aspect of alternative media. The paradox of their establishment is that at the very beginning of the alternative media there was VIVA radio which allowed Rostas to get into the broad public awareness. His following project, the magazine Zem a Vek, also went on an untraditional journey for alternative media as an attempt to compete standard print periodicals on the market. The fact that a certain part of prominent figures from alternative scene have experience in working in mainstream media is less surprising. These are Rostas from Zem a Vek (TV Markíza)[178], Benka (Trend), Huďo (STV) and Kršiak with Koróni from Slobodný vysielač who coworked in Lumen radio.

4.3 From Pirated Radio to an Attempt for Area-Wide Television

Despite the fact that Zem a Vek (together with Mlčanie) and Slobodný vysielač were projects of two different groups of people, cooperation between these two projects may be noticed in some spheres from the beginning. For instance, in regard to their mutual barter advertising. Ľubomír Huďo who was active as a foreign-political presenter in various print periodicals and from 1996 as a president of foreign news service of public

---

177 „Mediálne.sk: Z Banskej Bystrice sa (opäť) ozve Slobodný vysielač."
178 „Vrtí pes chvostom alebo chvost psom?"

service STV (Slovak television), he was even active simultaneously in both media – contributed to Zem a vek and in Slobodný vysielač and together with Norbert Lichtner, they had their own program called Informačná vojna (Information War) prior to his entry to alternative media. The name and also format of this program is markedly similar to the program Infowars by Alex Jones[179] – a prominent figure of alternative media in the United States. In this period an activist Peter Baďura is provided with his own space in broadcasting of Slobodný vysielač[180] and was linked to the branch of Indymedia and an attempt to publish the daily Verejnosť.

We find the period of 2013–2014 as an expansion of alternative media – the listening rate of Slobodné rádio ranges from thirty up to sixty thousand listeners[181], listener success of Mlčanie was reflected in sales of the book with the same name and until 2014 the circulation increased from original five thousand to twenty up to twenty-five thousand, returned copies representing about 10% according to the data.[182] The number of subscribers ranges from six to seven thousand[183]what enabled to publish the magazine without advertising according to its publisher. The magazine which context is created by nine skeleton editors and several external correspondents (figure from August 2014)[184] is published monthly in quality paper with professional photographs and elegant graphics. The editorial staff also launch a website that is not a base of their publication activities though. During several months, the magazine also increases its size initially to 140[185] pages later on currently to 148 pages[186]. The subtitle on the magazine cover also changes. The original *"Hidden Information without Censorship"* is replaced with *"Geopolitical and Cultural Monthly"*[187]. The magazine content may be divided into three groups: social-political (with an emphasis on abroad), cultural and "green." The last one has excessively

---

179 „Infowars.com."
180 „Protiprud.sk: Články autora Peter Sanve."
181 „tyzden.sk: Planéta Rostas."
182 „Havranovo talk show, hostia: Tibor Eliot Rostas a Juraj Smatana."
183 „HNonline.sk: Aj Slovákov zaplavuje ruská propaganda."
184 „zemavek.sk: Archív časopisov – august 2014."
185 „zemavek.sk: Archív časopisov – február 2015."
186 „zemavek.sk: Archív časopisov – január 2016."
187 „zemavek.sk: Archív časopisov – február 2015."

broad range – from communities across Europe that try to live out of civilization, healing effects of herbs through chemicals in food stuff and advice how to survive in nature. These groups are supplemented by an editorial by the chief editor, the theme of the month, interview, and both domestic and foreign news overview or news reports.

The listening rate of Slobodný vysielač in February 2014 ranged from thirty to sixty thousand listeners[188]. Certain image on the listening rate of the radio especially among young people is provided by data from the application Radia.sk that monitors listening rate of radio through mobile devices. According to the date from this application, Slobodný vysielač belonged to 20 most-listened stations in September 2014. Nowadays, it has its stable position in TOP 10.[189]

Program structure of the radio was relatively varied from its beginning – variety of broadcasted formats was however reflected on their periodicity – some programs were broadcasted once or twice a month, other had irregular periodicity. At the beginning, the part of the daily program, particularly in February 2013[190] were 10 blocks, two of them were rebroadcasts (News of Slobodný vysielač) and the second block consisted of rebroadcasted program according to own choice). The radio Slobodný vysielač focuses only on the Internet – it uses it for spreading its broadcasting and actively works with social media websites compared to Zem a vek. Attendance of the individual websites was not successfully found out in this period because they are not included in attendance monitoring together with websites of mainstream media.

Important moment happened in June 2015 when the chief editor of Zem a vek Tibor Rostas and a member of the editorial staff Dušan Budzák visited an editorial office of the magazine *Meždunarodnaja žizň* where they negotiated on possible cooperation and support of the project of the media

---

188 „tyzden.sk: Planéta Rostas."
189 This research is limited because it involves only data from the application Radia.sk Application was downloaded and installed almost for 240 times until the end of 2016 and it is used by more than 23 thousand listeners monthly.
190 Slobodný vysielač's Facebook page, Accessed December 5, 2016, https://www.facebook.com/SlobodnyVysielac/posts/422198294532999.

house in Slovakia with potential range within V4 countries[191]. Following medialization of this negotiation resulted in movements in alternative media. Ľubomír Huďo left the editorial office of Zem a vek as a protest against these negotiations. A co-founder of Slobodný vysielač Norbert Lichtner dealt with his long-term dissatisfaction with the situation in the radio in a similar way a few days later. A few months later the couple tried to run a TV station called IN TV. It was not established by granting a license but by transformation from already existing regional television TV Karpaty. The Council for Broadcasting and Retransmission decided on the change of the name in September 2015.[192]

We mention IN TV in regard to alternative media due to the character of the news service it was supposed to provide viewers with. At the beginning, owners, however, did not present their intention to deflect from the character of a typical mainstream media, yet the news service should have been provided by the association of Huďa and Lichtner Infovojna. The intention was therefore similar as in the case of Rostas's Mlčanie – to get an alternative format into mainstream media. It is also confirmed in an appeal on the website Infovojna that asked the public for financial support for *"the first independent news service team acting in the Slovak mainstream.*[193] These efforts were reflected in the names of the programs that were supposed to be provided by OZ Infovojna to IN TV. Main news service program was called Information War: *Non-mainstream View on Events in Society*. Besides Informačná vojna Norbert Lichtner hosted also next news service program called *Foreign News Service without Political Correctness*. Lichtner together with Huďo later through OZ Infovojna got into the ownership structures of the television[194].

The project seemed promising; from December 2015, IN TV was in a testing operation and a former presenter Martina Šimkovičová became one

---

191 „interaffairs.ru: Zhurnalisty iz Slovakii Dusan Budzak i Tibor Rostas – gosti zhurnala Mezdunarodnaya zhizn."
192 „medialne.sk: Televízia IN TV sa chystá na štart. Správy dodá moderátor Slobodného vysielača."
193 „mediálne.trend.sk: IN TV sa chystá na štart."
194 „Výpis z obchodného registra Okresného súdu Bratislava I."

of its prominent figures[195]. In February 2016, IN TV even organized several pre-electoral discussions used for launching the testing digital broadcasting through ground transmitters[196]. They were gradually involved in the offers of some cable operators and launching began on 13 April; yet after the first week of broadcasting, the news service no longer occurred in broadcasting only on social media. Simultaneously, the entire television got into trouble, and the planned full format broadcasting was never launched. Majority of the operators excluded IN TV from their offer by August.[197]

After the failure of IN TV project, Huďo and Lichtner continued with production of Informačná vojna. Later the program creators decided to establish their own Internet radio Infovojna that broadcasts only eight programs by Huďo and Lichtner though. Informačná vojna is on the air generally every working day in late afternoon. A record is then spread through YouTube portal and social media websites.[198]

In November 2016, a deeper cooperation of alternative media began. Individual projects which cooperation was so far limited to barter advertising or providing space for author products were now merged into association of so-called Association of Independent Media (ANM). Association was established by five media that classify themselves as alternative – Zem a vek, Slobodný vysielač, Hlavné správy and Internet portals, Medzičas and DAV DVA. According to its founders, the activity of ANM should be based on three pillars:

1. Sending a signal to readers and listeners that these media strive for common course of actions while defending the institute of freedom of speech and expression.
2. Protection of individual membership media and their coworkers against attacks and defaming by various *"activists"* and mainstream media. If necessary, the Association will use legal means as well.

---

195 „Medialne.sk: Televízia IN TV sa chystá na štart. Správy dodá moderátor Slobodného vysielača."
196 „Medialne.sk: „IN TV chce spustiť celodenné vysielanie do konca marca."
197 „Omediach.com: Bublina okolo IN TV spľasla."
198 „Infovojna.sk: Archív."

Image 13: Print screen from the web site of the journal Zem & Vek with the information about the foundation of Association of Independent Media from 02/12/2016 (http://zemavek.sk/vznikla-asociacia-nezavislych-medii/)

3. An ambition to enter legislative procedures and give statements to draft laws regarding media.[199]

4.4 Criticism of Alternative Media

Alternative media in Slovakia has been criticized for a long time in Slovakia – for non-professionalism, publishing of conspiracy theories and untruths, providing space for statements on the verge of extremism or for spreading so-called Russian propaganda.

Although at the beginning of their functioning, almost no critical responses are noticed. During this period, the attention of mainstream

---

199 Zem a vek: *Vznikla Asociácia nezávislých médií*

media may be referred to as sporadic – only left-wing portal jetotak.sk[200] noticed the activity of alternative media until 2014. The change started in 2014 and through the escalation of tension in Ukraine that led to armed conflict. The difference was markedly demonstrated between traditional and alternative media in regard to providing information about events in Ukraine. Later this difference interferes into other topics especially foreign political – not only the war in Syria and presidential elections in the United States but also domestic ones such as the activities of the North Atlantic Alliance in Slovakia. Throughout the year 2014, spreading and fight with so-called Russian propaganda that is supposed to be goal-directed, systematic and financed by Russian government structures also began to be discussed in Slovakia. It is alternative media that should be its medium.

In this period, criticism addressing alternative media – after jetotak.sk also priestori.sk[201] a.týždeň[202] publish their critical contributions.

A certain turning point in perceiving alternative media came when a civilian activist Juraj Smatana published a list of 42 websites that allegedly spread Russian propaganda afterwards. Since then the criticism of alternative media began to be more intense – media alternative is identified solely with spreading the mentioned propaganda from Russia. Not only media subsequently started to fight with this propaganda but non-governmental organizations established on transatlantic values, political parties and also the Ministry of Interior of the Slovak Republic find the Russian propaganda to be a threat.[203] Some of the mentioned subjects openly discuss the fact that propaganda in Slovakia is financially supported by structures of the Russian Federation.

To call websites from Juraj Smatana's list alternative would not be completely justified. There are also websites of various civil associations (Panslovanská únia), Church institutions (Byzantský patriarchát), extremist organizations (Vzdor Kysuce, Slovenské hnutie obrody), political parties

200 „Jetotak.sk: Vtáčkovia, siroty a blázni na rádiu Viva."
201 „Priestori.sk: Zem a vek nebezpečných konšpirácií."
202 „Tyzden.sk: Planéta Rostas."
203 „Dennikn.sk: Štát prvýkrát priznal, že ruská propaganda útočí na prozápadné smerovanie Slovenska."

(Magnificat Slovakia) or blogs by individuals – so websites regarding their nature could not have a character of a means of mass communication.

The definition of a term *"Russian propaganda"* being absent is also a negative aspect in this case. Despite the intensity of the usage of this term nobody has stated the boundary between legitimate political PR and propaganda.[204] This fact may also give an impression in the society that propaganda is only heading for Slovakia from one side respectively and that the West does not produce any propaganda. Such a concept is incorrect and it paradoxically provides an opportunity for a creation of a conspiracy theory based on the fact that spread and financially supported goal-directed campaign through alternative media is also spread in Slovakia instructed by the highest governmental posts in Russia. Such statements polarize the society and to a certain extent they result in ostracism of non-conforming groups and individuals. For instance, throughout the year 2015, there were many appeals by mainstream media in order to disqualify activists' and politicians' long-term criticizing of the North Atlantic Alliance from the public space.[205]

We will state several examples of inaccurateness in alternative media in the following pages. Due to the limited space, we will not describe examples of all slips in the period determined in advance, but regarding selected media, we will state one illustrative example of inaccurateness we have noticed about the readers/listeners.

4.4.1 Example 1: Slobodný vysielač: Overestimating the unemployment rate in the United States

A blogger Peter Farárik informed about the case of misleading on the air of Slobodný vysielač in December 2014.[206] On 5 December 2014, in a program hosted by Norbert Lichtner and Ľubomír Huďo, Audi alteram partem presenters were discussing an article from The New York Times that states that there are 321 thousand new vacancies in the United States.

---

204 Bekmatov, „*Dva svety – dve pravdy: Propaganda v 21. storočí,*" 175.
205 Ibid., 185.
206 Slobodný vysielač: Neschopnosť alebo cielené šírenie nezmyslov?"

"The New York Times greatly celebrated, there are 321 thousand new vacancies in the USA. Excellent number – *321 thousand vacancies and these are, indeed, real numbers provided by the Bureau of Labor. I say to myself: "The New York Times would definitely not lie." And it did not. It is true- in America there are 321 new vacancies. I say to myself they will not lie but they certainly hide something. So I started to dig into statistics and I made that effort, and so in the USA the statistics is not done in a way like- the employed- not employed but they do it in way that "the employed" and "not employed actively looking for a job" and "the unemployed not looking for a job". These are two such groups. Well and out of 330 million of residents where there are, indeed, plenty of the retired and children- now listen to me very carefully- so the New York Times is celebrating 321 thousand new vacancies, in the USA there are 92 million 447 thousand people who do not work towards the end of November of 2014. These are people who do not have a job and would like to have one and also people who will never look for a job. And now take that three hundred thousand number, so 92 million 100 thousand into consideration and that makes a difference. Since Obama has taken his office, 11 million 918 thousand vacancies were canceled. Almost 12 million of the American lost their jobs and now the New York Times is celebrating some sort of 321 thousand new vacancies. This is how propaganda is made."*[207]

As the blogger informed, the presenter uses expressively emotional intonation when he speaks about "great celebrating" or "hiding" by The New York Times. The presenter made a more serious slip while wrongly interpreting the numbers. The fact is that at the end of November 2014, there were not 330 million residents in the United States but 319 666 141.[208] Moreover, the data about the overall number of the unemployed (92 million 447 thousand) include also people who already cannot work at present (children and the retired), actually not unemployed people. In November 2014, there were not 92 million of them as Lichtner states but only about 6 545 000 which is approximately 5.8%.[209]

4.4.2 Example 2: Zem a vek: Doubting the effects of chemotherapy

In 2014, in the November issue in particular, the topic of the month in Zem a vek was cancer treatment. The editorial office chose a very suggestive

---

207 „Audi alteram partem 05.12.2014 Ľubomír Huďo."
208 "US Census Bureau."
209 "Bureau of labour statistics."

headline for the cover of the magazine: *"The war with cancer is fraud."* The magazine brought several articles mainly about people who deal with cancer treatment but each of them in a different way. The reader was offered an opportunity to read about the treatment, mitigation of the disease respectively by so-called holistic (overall) approach, by detoxification or even by fruit and vegetable juices. Each of the operators was given some space in a separate article with an extent to about one double page. The editorial staff provided space for an eight-page interview also to a prominent oncologist Ján Lakot, and not only Slovak (Hospodárske noviny) but foreign (Cable News Network, CNN) mainstream media informed in the past about his research activity.

Besides these, Tibor Rostas contributed to the topic of the month by a vast almost six-page article. It was this article that became the subject of criticism. A blogger, Marián Jonáš, a general practitioner, pointed out at insufficient handling of facts, especially with numbers.[210] The blogger reproached the chief editor with three things:

1. argumentation with the results of a research that are out of context – an author of the article refers to a survey stating that out of 118 oncologists the vast majority neither would undergo chemotherapy nor recommend it to their close people. What was not mentioned is the fact that the survey was done in 1986 and it refers only to one specific type of cancer and following a way of treatment that was not sufficiently tested in 1986;
2. a wrong interpretation of another research – according to M. Jánoš, the author wrongly stated percentage data referring to the contribution of the additional treatment that prolonged patients' lives as the percentage of patients who survived five-year period after chemotherapy treatment;
3. not stating all information available – an author refers to Chris Wark as an example of a man who refused traditional treatment yet he cured himself, thanks to alternative methods. The fact that Wark refused chemotherapy as a supplement to surgical tumor removal that he underwent is missing.

---

210 „Tibor E. Rostas šíri nebezpečné klamstvá o liečbe rakoviny."

The exchange of reactions between the editorial staff and blogger followed until the editorial staff addressed the mentioned doctor Lakota who on one hand refused statements that Zem a vek would discourage patients from doctor's appointment but on the other hand informed about the fact that some information *"was not very accurate."* He therefore also decided to provide a vast interview and possibility of consultations with him to *"to clear the inaccuracies" and "correct some things."*[211]

For information completeness, we state a short text that opens the topic of the month in Zem a vek: *"We are fully aware of the fact that cancer is one of the most serious themes. It is not possible to comprehend it in a single issue and at the same time it is not possible to draw clear statements and conclusions. Human organism, life, disease and death are still in many aspects a big unknown for experts as well as for people looking for alternative ways of treatment. Every third of us will succumb to this disease. Cancer is, however, a prospering industry. In Slovakia itself, the annual costs for its treatment exceeded one billion euros while this treatment and therapies have in majority of the most common types of canes literally zero treatment success. It is immensely important to approach this serious disease from many aspects. Cancer is commonly a lethal disease so therefore- or right because of this-it forces us to think of our fate and to often re-evaluate everything that formed our seemingly carefree live till then."*[212]

Despite the fact that this text declares an effort of the editorial staff to keep distance and on top of all things the question if they succeeded remains open – on one hand, there are non-scientific procedures of treatment or an article by the chief director with a suggestive title, and on the other hand, there is an interview with a prominent oncologist and his statements that such articles have no influence on attendance of patients at their doctors'.

The aim of this chapter was not to deny the inaccurateness of alternative media. In many aspects, the criticism is justifiable – the lower ability to handle facts and data (partially resulting from low professionalism of journalists – only a small amount of alternative media employ journalists full-time as mainstream media do) or tendencies to incline to conspiracy

---

211 „MUDR. Lakota: Nikde som sa nestretol s tým, že by Zem a Vek odrádzal od návštevy lekára."
212 „Téma mesiaca: Boj s rakovinou je podvod," 25.

theories (to a certain extent, determined by the personality of a given journalists – critics of the magazine Zem a vek, for instance, pointed out at the occurrence of conspiracy theories only in articles by selected journalists while articles written by other journalists are avoided). The problematic aspect is creating a space for extremist opinions. Especially Slobodný vysielač which fundamental philosophy is to provide a space for all opinions that do not appear in mainstream has been criticized several times for allowing the right-wing extremist organizations to perform, and similar opinion tendencies were demonstrated multiple times at selected presenters . On the other side, the station also has a program in its broadcasting dealing with opinions of the left wing, especially a radical one.

Although in regard to spreading of Russian propaganda, so-called *pro-Russian narrative* is definitely present in alternative media. The cause of its presence, however, may not be reasoned by unfounded statements about a disinformation campaign by Russia but rather by the fact that in the past years the biggest opinion differences were created in the area of geopolitics on the axis Russia – the West. Since crucial events also lie on this axis which influenced Europe (war in Syria and following migration wave, crisis in Ukraine that led to war, etc.), it is logical that people with different word-views on understanding geopolitical situation started to recruit to the alternative information.[213]

Eventually, the content of alternative media does not solely consist of conspiracy theories and alleged Russian propaganda – these are only the products heavily criticized by the mainstream.

Slobodný vysielač has many formats in its offer that are not *"mainstream defective"* (health, economics, folklore, living, consulting, cinematography, literature...) despite their alternative profiling. The same may be said about the individual sections of Zem and vek that, for instance, focus on traveling, music and book tips, health, and reportages about ordinary people or legal consulting. We would also find media products that may be attractive for

---

213 Several analysts assume that after D. Trump's commencement the tension resulting from relationship between the United States and Russia will impact the relationship between the United States and China. It may therefore be assumed that after the phrase "Russian propaganda," the phrase "Chinese propaganda" began to be discussed more intensively.

mainstream viewer (mapping of communities across Europe that decided to live on their own or reportages from "hot places" of Ukrainian crisis).

In accordance with information stated in the part referring to definitions of alternative media, it is necessary to be aware of the fact that alternative media are mostly of strong opinions that present their definition more openly and it is not uncommon that they tend to motivate their auditorium to participation in social changes respectively.[214] To achieve this, they raise topics and questions that are beyond mainstream discourse.[215]

At times of bipolar split of the world, the term "information war" was frequented and it is currently coming back to public discussion – not only in alternative media but also in statements of mainstream journalists, analysts or even from the mouth of the President of the Slovak Republic. For better understanding of functioning of mainstream and alternative media, the thesis about information war itself may be helpful. Mainstream media are allowed to wage a war on a long-term basis along the full length of imaginary front, that is, they constantly inform about all events from many spheres regardless of their resulting reader or viewer effect. On the other hand, alternative media are mostly dependent on guerrilla way of fight. It is based on the selection of topics that, in a form of irregular published outcomes and in combination with sometimes exaggerating language, have a change to succeed in competitive fight for a reader, listener or viewer with the mainstream.

4.5 Summary

We demonstrated in a chronological order that alternative media in Slovakia despite their short acting on media market were able to make a significant response of public audience as well as mainstream media. In regard to a limited size of media market, it is possible to determine that the content of Slovak alternative is based on diversity of views in geopolitical events.

Alternative media against the mainstream media in any form (community media, financially and power independent, radical, non-conform) means

---

214 Waltz, Alternative and activist media, 3–4.
215 Willett, "The State of Alternative Publishing in America: Issues and Implications for Libraries," 14.

spreading of opinion plurality, and therefore its existence may be found beneficial in Slovakia. However, there are two fundamental questions ahead of Slovak alternative – how to increase the professionalism of its journalists and where the tolerance limit is in its content.

Serious slips connected to the production of its content which accompany the alternative media are possibly eliminated, and efforts to suppress them should be in the public interest. There are several ways where to begin – and it necessarily does not have to be only editorial offices of alternative media but universities as well. As an example, we can mention The Faculty of Social Sciences, Charles University in Prague that offers also a subject called Alternative media in the program of Media Studies. Such a subject in a study plan of future journalists may help to better understand the issue of alternative journalism. If we take the fact that alternative media often provide their coworkers with greater range of personal autonomy into consideration, then it may be assumed that the new generation of journalists of alternative media that could also be recruited from graduates in mass media or journalist program could positively influence the level of professionalism of alternative media.

The second issue that concerns alternative media in Slovakia is how to deal with penetration of extremist opinions into its context. Regarding Slovakia, it is especially right-wing extremism demonstrated by the attempts to doubt holocaust or racist and xenophobic tendencies. The nature of alternative media is based on creating space for opinions and topics that are ignored by the mainstream – where is the limit of the tolerance shifted though? Should alternative media be regulated? How to approach this issue in a situation when mainstream media are also forced to provide a space for politicians with extremist opinions (members of the parliament)? The clear limit (however shifted compared to the mainstream) of the tolerance in the alternative with a focus on extremism should definitely exist. A positive role in the process of setting this limit could be especially played by organizations uniting alternative media such as the Association of Independent Media. Alternative media could create their own control mechanisms independent from mainstream with their help.

Conclusion

As we have stated in Introduction, this monograph identifies and explains the most significant challenges that Slovak Mass Media nowadays face. Every chapter is focused on one specified problem related to the media and on the analysis of current media output or by analyzing the conditions within which the media in Slovakia work. It demonstrates how the problems of actual media communication are reflected. What is common for all of the identified problematic matters is specific social and political atmosphere in which the Slovak media system has evolved. In democracy, Slovak media operated a little longer than 28 years, but modern Slovak media system is existing for only 24 years (from 1993). First public service Slovak broadcaster has been established in 1991. Maybe 20 years or more of existence of some institution looks like quite a long period; however, it is not enough time for achieving adequate knowledge and experience, solving the everyday problems and training new generation of journalists unburdened by the past.

The media nowadays are more effective in regard to control authorities and their exercise of power than the media in the nineties of the 20th century, and the corruption is considered by media as a rather serious problem of our society. Current Slovak media more consistently cover the theme of corruption (and other themes related to the exercise of power) in their news, and the increase of relevant results are significant. However, this statement is valid in relation with the tradition media; Internet media are focused mainly on soft news taken from social networks or other media.

The biggest challenge for media in future will be looking for the models on how to convince the public that their work is worth to be trusted. The authors of this monograph see a solution by increasing the professionalism and quality of the work of journalists, focusing on the serious and important themes, deepening investigative work and respecting ethical request of journalism. Simultaneously by the traditional functions of media, nowadays it is necessary that media shall reflect their integration function as an effective instrument against social exclusion, stereotyping and prejudice. This role of media is being more important in the context of increasing the extremism, nationalism and hate which is witnessed by all in Europe. Specific task of supporting the media literacy education and awareness of citizens lies on the media of public service. PSM are one of the mechanisms how to guarantee the public access to relevant information prepared with the sense of responsibility. The increase of viewership can indicate that in Slovakia public has the confidence in public service media; however, also in Slovakia public broadcaster faces the disinterest from youth. This is the reason why public broadcaster must constantly seek ways how to obtain the attention of young generation, mainly by incorporating new technologies in broadcasting, making the program more available not only in real broadcasting time but anytime and everywhere.

Another significant challenge of these days is to secure the plurality of information. Media market represented by mainstream media, as a market in which quite high concentration and monopolization is evident, cannot guarantee that any more. The solution may be offered by alternative media. However, they have to settle their rules on how to deal with (or rather get rid of) the extremist opinions. The author of the fourth chapter offers the idea on how to do this – to create an independent institution or association that will define the ethical rules of alternative media work and to include the specialized studying program of alternative media within the existing university studies of journalism and mass media communication.

Finally, in regard to thoughts and conclusions referred in this monograph, we suppose that it is necessary to support education in the area of media literacy and indoctrination of moral values and humanity. Only the individual who has the ability to consider and to critically evaluate the presented information as important, objective and verified (or not), is able to make the decision that is relevant for his or her life, happiness and realization in society.

Bibliography

Cited References

"Boris Kollár's Facebook page." Facebook.com. Last modified May, 15, 2016.

„Dôvodová správa k zákonu č. 340/2012 Z.z. o úhrade za služby verejnosti poskytované Rozhlasom a televíziou Slovenska a o zmene a doplnení niektorých zákonov." Accessed January 31, 2017. http://www.najpravo.sk/dovodove-spravy/rok-2012/340-2012-z-z.html

"Royal commission on the press. Periodicals and the alternative press", London: HMSO, 1977 in Atton, C. *Alternative media*. London: Sage, 2002.

"Slobodný vysielač's Facebook page." Accessed December 5, 2016. https://www.facebook.com/SlobodnyVysielac/posts/422198294532999

Abel, R. "*An alternative press. Why?*" *Publishing research quarterly* 12, no. 4 (1996): 78–84 in Atton, C. *Alternative media*. London: Sage, 2002.

Atelier.sk. „Vrtí pes chvostom alebo chvost psom?" Accessed December 20, 2016. http://www.attelier.sk/vrti-pes-chvostom-alebo-chvost-psom/

Atton, C. *Alternative media*. London: Sage, 2002.

Atton, C. *An alternative internet*. Edinburgh: Edinburgh University Press, 2004.

Atton, C. and J. Hamilton. *Alternative journalism*, London: Sage, 2008.

Bajomi-Lázár, P. and Á. Lampé. "Invisible Journalism? The Political Impact of Investigative Journalism in Hungary." *Media transformations*, vol. 9 (2013): 30–51.

BBC TV Licensing. "*Do you need a TV licence?*", BBC (2016): online. http://www.tvlicensing.co.uk/about/foi-legal-framework-AB16 (accessed January 31, 2017).

Bekmatov, A. „Dva svety – dve pravdy: propaganda v 21. storočí" In *Megatrendy & médiá 2016*, edited by Petranová, D. and S. Magál, 174–188. Trnava: FMK UCM v Trnave, 2016.

Benčík, J. „Lesk a bieda kurtizán konšpiračného mainstreamu." Accessed December 20, 2016 https://dennikn.sk/blog/lesk-bieda-kurtizan-konspiracneho-mainstreamu/.

Benedikovič, T., SITA. *The ban on journalists has been criticized.* Webnoviny (2017): online. https://www.webnoviny.sk/paska-rozvasnil-opoziciu-zakaz-pre-novinarov-zozal-kritiku/novinari-jpg-10/ (accessed February 13, 2018)

Benedikovičová, M. „*Šimečka: SME nehľadá pravdu.*" SME (2013): online. https://domov.sme.sk/c/6667070/simecka-sme-nehlada-pravdu. html (accessed January 31, 2017).

Brečka, S. „*Profesia: Novinár.*" Otázky žurnalistiky 49, no 3–4 (2006): 24–51.

Chmelár, E. *Uhorská tlačová politika (so zreteľom na slovenské novinárstvo).* Nitra: FF UKF v Nitre, 1998.

Chomsky, N. "The propaganda system." Accessed December 16, 2016. http://goodtimesweb.org/analysis/z-loot-chomsky-propaganda-system-may-1992.html

Council of Europe. Picture of Logo of Council of Europe. Council of Europe (2017): online. https://www.coe.int/documents/16695/994584/COE-Logo-Quadri.png/ee7b1fc6-055b-490b-a59b-a65969e440a2?t=1371222819000 (accessed January 7, 2018).

ČTK, pol. „*Vznikol slovenský tím pre Panama Papers. Kauza spojila novinárov.*" Mediálne (2016): online. http://medialne.etrend.sk/tlac/vznikol-slovensky-tim-pre-panama-papers-kauza-spojila-novinarov. html (accessed December 20, 2017).

Dahlgren, P. "The transformation of democracy?" In *New media and politics*, edited by Axford, B. and R. Huggins, 64–88. London: Sage Publications, 2001.

Downing, J. *Radical media: rebellious communication and social movements.* London: Sage, 2001.

Downing, J. *Radical media: the political experience of alternative communication.* Boston, MA: South End Press. 1984.

Downmunt, T., K. Coyer. *The alternative media handbook.* New York: Routledge, 2007.

Európska únia. „Amsterdamská zmluva." Accessed December 27, 2016. https://www.nrsr.sk/web/Static/sk-SK/EU/Doc/amsterdamska-zmluva. pdf.

Európska únia. „Smernica Európskeho parlamentu a Rady 2010/13/EÚ z 10. marca 2010 o koordinácii niektorých ustanovení upravených zákonom, iným právnym predpisom alebo správnym opatrením v členských štátoch týkajúcich sa poskytovania audiovizuálnych mediálnych služieb (smernica o audiovizuálnych mediálnych službách). Kodifikované znenie." Accessed December 27, 2016. http://eur-lex. europa.eu/legal-content/SK/TXT/PDF/?uri=CELEX:32010L0013&from=EN.

Európska únia. „Zmluva o fungovaní Európskej únie." In *Úradný vestník Európskej únie*, Zväzok 55, no. C 326, 2012.

Farárik, P. „Slobodný vysielač. Neschopnosť alebo cielené šírenie nezmyslov?" Accessed January 20, 2017. https://dennikn.sk/blog/slobodny-vysielac-neschopnost-alebo-cielene-sirenie-nezmyslov-2/.

Farenzeová, M., M. Kubánová and A. Salner. *Cestovná mapa pre riešenie problému nadmerného zastúpenia rómskych detí v špeciálnom školstve – analýza realistických krokov.* Bratislava: Slovak Governance Institut, 2013.

Felšoci, R., Plus 7 DNÍ weekly. *Slovaks do not treat the rights of Roma sufficiently.* Plus 7 DNÍ (2016): online. http://www.pluska.sk/fotogaleri a/?foto=&clanok=975420 (accessed January 5, 2018).

Galinski, A. „Zweierlei Perspektiven auf Gespräche: Ethnomethodologische Konversationsanalyse und Diskursanalyse im kontrastiven Vergleich." In *Linse, Linguistik-Server Essen.* Universität Duisburg-Essen, 2004. http://www.linse.uni-due.de/linse/esel/pdf/konversation_diskurs.pdf (accessed January 25, 2017).

Galmišová, D. *Kauzám sa najviac venujú v denníku SME.* Bratislava: Ineko, 2015.

Geissler, R. „Mediale Integration von ethnischen Minderheiten. Der Beitrag der Massenmedien zur interkulturellen Integration." In *Zur Rolle der Medien in der Einwanderungsgesellschaf, Wiso Diskurs,* edited by Fridrich, Ebert and Stiftung, 8–22. Bonn: Fridrich-Eber-Stiftungstr, 2010.

Glovičko, J. „*Kaliňák hovoril redaktorke Pravdy, čo má robiť.*" SME (2011): online. https://domov.sme.sk/c/6152656/kalinak-hovoril-redaktorke-pravdy-co-ma-robit.html (accessed February 2, 2017).

Gundelroy, M. "Glossary." Accessed December 16, 2016. http://www.gyrofrog.com/glossary-ff44.php

Hallin, D.C. and P. Mancini. *Systémy médií v postmoderním světe.* Praha: Portál, 2008.

Hamilton, J. "*Alternative media: Conceptual difficulties, critical possibilities,*" Journal of Communication Inquiry 24, no. 4 (2000): 357–378. http://journals.sagepub.com/doi/pdf/10.1177/0196859900024004002 (accessed January 20, 2017)

Infovojna. „infovojna.sk: Archív" http://www.infovojna.sk/archiv (accessed January 7, 2017).

Infowars. „infowars.com" http://www.infowars.com/ (accessed January 10, 2017).

Jakubčo, J., SITA. *SDKÚ has a plan how to put an end to "black" constructions.* Webnoviny (2017), https://www.webnoviny.sk/fotogaleria/sdku-ma-plan-ako-skoncovat-s-ciernymi-stavbami/?id=3 (accessed January 5, 2018)

Jakubowicz, K. "A New Promise for Public Service Provision in the Information Society". In *Media freedom and pluralism,* edited by B. Klimkiewicz, 193–227. Budapešť: Central European University Press, 2010. http://books.openedition.org/ceup/2177 (accessed December 17, 2016).

Jakubowicz, K. „Nová média a demokracie". In *Nová ekologie médií: Konvergence a mediamorfóza,* edited by K. Jakubowicz, 223–270. Zlín: VeRBuM, 2013.

Jánoš, M. „Tibor E. Rostas šíri nebezpečné klamstvá o liečbe rakoviny." Accessed December 15, 2016. https://dennikn.sk/blog/tibor-e-rostas-siri-nebezpecne-klamstva-o-rakovine/.

Jirák, J. and B. Köpplová. *Masová média.* Praha: Portál, 2009.

Kalenborn, C. and C. Lessmann, "The Impact of Democracy and Press Freedom on Corruption: Conditionality Matters." In *Journal of Policy Modeling* 6, no 35 (2013): 857–886.

Kostolný, M. „*Prečo odchádzame z denníka SME.*" Opentat.sk (2015): online. http://www.opentat.sk/post/99715656100/pre%C4%8Do-odch%C3%A1dzame-z-denn%C3%ADka-sme (accessed February 2, 2017).

Kranich, A. "*A question of balance: the role of libraries in providing alternatives to the mainstream media.*" Collection Building 19, no. 3 (2000): 85–91.

Krejčí, O. *Politická psychologie.* Praha: Ekopress, 2004.

Kubánová, M. „Keď jediná škola v obci je len pre postihnuté deti." Sme. sk. (2016): online. https://komentare.sme.sk/c/20140682/ked-jedina-skola-v-obci-je-len-pre-mentalne-postihnute-deti.html (accessed January 25, 2017).

Leggewie, C. „Demokratie auf der Datenautobahn." In *Internet und Politik. Von der Zuschauer – zur Beteiligungsdemokratie*, edited by Leggewie C. and C. Maar, 15–54. Mannheim: 1998, http://politik-digital.de/news/demokratie_auf_der_datenautobahn-601/ (accessed January 25, 2017).

Lincényi, M. and G. Tamene "The media as public opinion leader in influencing and setting policy: the case of Slovakia." In *Journal on Law, Economy & Management*. London: STS Science Centre, 2013. vol. 3, no. 1, 95–99.

Mafra Slovakia. „HNonline.sk: Aj Slovákov zaplavuje ruská propaganda." Accessed December 18, 2016. http://dennik.hnonline.sk/svet/519076-aj-slovakov-zaplavuje-ruska-propaganda.

McChesney, R.W. *Problém médií. Jak uvažovat o dnešních médiích*. Všeň: Grimmus, 2009.

McGinnis, J. O. *Accelerating democracy: Transforming governance through technology*. Princeton & Oxford: Princeton University Press, 2013.

McQuail, D. *Úvod do teorie masové komunikace*. 4th ed. Praha: Portál, 2009.

Media watch dog. „Mediawatch.dog: Viete prví: Vznikla nová televízia IN TV. Stojí za ňou zakladateľ rádia Slobodný vysielač Norbert Lichtner (aktualizované)." Accessed January 6, 2016. http://www.mediawatch.dog/viete-prvi-vznikla-nova-televizia-in-tv-stoji-za-nou-zakladatel-radia-slobodny-vysielac-norbert-lichtner/

Median.sk. *MML – TGI, národný prieskum spotreby, médií, a životného štýlu, Market & Media & Lifestyle – TGI*. Bratislava: MEDIAN.SK, 2012. http://www.median.sk/sk/mml-tgi/ (accessed December 5, 2016).

Median.sk. *MML – TGI, národný prieskum spotreby, médií, a životného štýlu, Market & Media & Lifestyle – TGI*. Bratislava: MEDIAN.SK, 2016. http://www.median.sk/sk/mml-tgi/ (accessed December 5, 2016).

Meyer, T. „Die Theatralität der Politik in der Mediendemokratie." In *Aus Politik und Zeitgeschichte. Beilage zur Wochenzeitung Das Parlament 53*, no. 53 (2003): 12–19.

Mikloš, I. „Správa o boji proti korupcii na Slovensku." In *Korupcia na Slovensku a jej spracovanie v médiách*, edited by Nagyová, I. and E. Žitňanský, 10–25. Bratislava: Róbert Vico-vydavateľstvo, 2001.

Mikulka, M. „*Spolumajitel Penty Dospiva: Chceme mediální štít proti iracionálním útokům.*" Hospodářské noviny (2015): online. http://archiv.ihned.cz/c1-63893810-spolumajitel-penty-dospiva-chceme-medialni-stit-proti-iracionalnim-utokum (accessed February 3, 2017).

Minárik, M. „*Media and Demokracy in Slovakia*" (Master thesis, University of Glasgow, 2000).

Ministerstvo innostrannych del RF. „interaffairs.ru: Zhurnalisty iz Slovakii Dusan Budzak i Tibor Rostas – gosti zhurnala Mezdunarodnaya zhizn." Accessed January 3, 2017. https://interaffairs.ru/news/show/13319.

Ministerstvo spravodlivosti SR. „Výpis z obchodného registra Okresného súdu Bratislava I" Accessed February 20, 2017. http://www.orsr.sk/vypis.asp?ID=333147&SID=2&P=1.

Mintz, M. „Prečo je investigatívna žurnalistika nedocenená a precenená zároveň," In *Korupcia na Slovensku a jej spracovanie v médiách*, edited by Nagyová, I. and E. Žitňanský, 118–138. Bratislava: Róbert Vico-vydavateľstvo, 2001.

Mrvová, I. „*Exšéf IPI: Naši novinári si kontrolu moci pomýlili s bezbrehou kritikou.*" Stratégie (2016): online. http://strategie.hnonline.sk/media/891852-exsef-ipi-novinari-si-pomylili-kontrolu-moci-s-bezbrehou-kritikou (accessed January 30, 2017).

N press. „Proruskú propagandu o zhýralom Západe u nás šíri 42 webov." Accessed January 10, 2017. https://dennikn.sk/57740/prorusku-propagandu-o-zhyralom-zapade-u-nas-siri-42-webov/

N press. „Štát prvýkrát priznal, že ruská propaganda útočí na prozápadné smerovanie Slovenska." Accessed January 10, 2017. https://dennikn.sk/481082/stat-prvykrat-priznal-ze-ruska-propaganda-utoci-prozapadne-smerovanie-slovenska/.

News and media holding, „medialne.trend.sk: Televízia IN TV sa chystá na štart." Accessed November 2, 2016. http://medialne.etrend.sk/

televizia/in-tv-sa-chysta-na-start-hlavne-spravodajstvo-bude-od-moderatora-slobodneho-vysielaca.html.

News and media holding. „medialne.trend.sk: IN TV chce spustiť celodenné vysielanie do konca marca." Accessed January 6, 2017. https://medialne.etrend.sk/televizia/in-tv-celodenne-vysielanie-spustime-do-konca-marca.html.

News and media holding. „medialne.trend.sk: Z Banskej Bystrice sa (opäť) ozve Slobodný vysielač." Accessed December 11, 2016. http://medialne.etrend.sk/radia-tlacove-spravy/z-banskej-bystrice-sa-opat-ozve-slobodny-vysielac.html.

Newton Media. *Mediálna analýza pre Romano Kher – Rómsky dom: 1. júl–31. október 2016.* Bratislava: Newton Media, 2016. http://romanokher.eu/wp-content/uploads/2016/12/Medialna_analyza_Romsky_dom_2016.pdf (accessed January 25, 2017).

Newton media. *Rómovia, novinári a médiá: Mediálna analýza: 1. Júl–30. November 2014.* Bratislava: Newton Media, 2014. http://romanokher.eu/wp-content/uploads/2014/12/Medialny-obraz-Romov.pdf (accessed January 25, 2017).

Nicholson, T. „Investigatívna žurnalistika na Slovensku: nátlak na zneváženie etiky." In *Korupcia na Slovensku a jej spracovanie v médiách*, edited by Nagyová, I. and E. Žitňanský, 103–105. Bratislava: Róbert Vico-vydavateľstvo, 2001.

Nicholson, T. *Gorila.* Bratislava: Dixit, 2012.

Noam, E. M. „Digittaler Schwindel." Accessed January 25, 2017. http://politik-digital.de/news/digitaler_schwindel-594/.

NR SR. „Zákon č. 254/1991 Zb. o Slovenskej televízii." Accessed December 1, 2016. https://www.slov-lex.sk/pravne-predpisy/SK/ZZ/1991/254/vyhlasene_znenie.html.

NR SR. „Zákon č. 255/1991 Zb. o Slovenskom rozhlase." Accessed December 1, 2016. https://www.slov-lex.sk/pravne-predpisy/SK/ZZ/1991/255/vyhlasene_znenie.html.

NR SR. „Zákon č. 308/2000 Z.z.o vysielaní a retransmisii a o zmene zákona č. 195/2000 Z. z. o telekomunikáciách." Accessed December 1, 2016. https://www.slov-lex.sk/pravne-predpisy/SK/ZZ/2000/308/20160701.

NR SR. „Zákon č. 340/2012 Z.z. o úhrade za služby verejnosti poskytované Rozhlasom a televíziou Slovenska a o zmene a doplnení

niektorých zákonov." Accessed January 31, 2017. https://www.slov-lex.
sk/pravne-predpisy/SK/ZZ/2012/340/20160701.

NR SR. „Zákon č. 482/1992 Zb., ktorým sa mení a dopĺňa zákon
Slovenskej národnej rady č. 254/1991 Zb. o Slovenskej televízii."
Accessed January 12, 2017. https://www.slov-lex.sk/pravne-predpisy/
SK/ZZ/1992/482/19921026.

NR SR. „Zákon č. 483/1992 Zb. ktorým sa mení a dopĺňa zákon
Slovenskej národnej rady č. 255/1991 Zb. o Slovenskom rozhlase."
Accessed December 1, 2016. https://www.slov-lex.sk/pravne-predpisy/
SK/ZZ/1992/483/19921026.

NR SR. „Zákon č. 532/2010 Z.z. o Rozhlase a televízii Slovenska a o
zmene a doplnení niektorých zákonov." Accessed January 12, 2017.
https://www.slov-lex.sk/pravne-predpisy/SK/ZZ/2010/532/20140101.

NR SR. „Zákon, ktorým sa mení a dopĺňa zákon č. 340/2012 Z. z.
o úhrade za služby verejnosti poskytované Rozhlasom a televíziou
Slovenska a o zmene a doplnení niektorých zákonov v znení neskorších
predpisov a ktorým sa mení a dopĺňa zákon č. 532/2010 Z. z. o
Rozhlase a televízii Slovenska a o zmene a doplnení niektorých zákonov
v znení neskorších predpisov." Accessed January 31, 2017. https://
www.slov-lex.sk/legislativne-procesy?p_p_id=processDetail_WAR_
portletsel&p_p_lifecycle=0&p_p_state=normal&p_p_mode=view&p_p_
col_id=column-2&p_p_col_count=1&_processDetail_WAR_portletsel_
startact=1463485044000&_processDetail_WAR_portletsel_idact=10&_
processDetail_WAR_portletsel_action=files&_processDetail_WAR_
portletsel_cisloLP=LP%2F2016%2F446.

O médiách. „omediach.com: Bublina okolo IN TV spľasla." Accessed
January 6, 2017. http://www.omediach.com/tv/item/9459-bublina-
okolo-intv-splasla.

OECD. *PISA 2012 Results in Focus: What 15-year-olds know and what
they can do with what they know.* Pisa: OECD, 2014. http://www.oecd.
org/pisa/keyfindings/pisa-2012-results-overview.pdf (accessed January
25, 2017).

ORF. „Gebühren Info Service". Accessed January 30, 2017. https://www.
gis.at/fremdsprachen/english/.

Panta rhei. „pantarhei.sk: Eseje, úvahy štúdie – Mlčanie II." Accessed
February 20, 2017. http://www.pantarhei.sk/knihy/beletria/eseje-uvahy-
studie/mlcanie-ii.html.

Panta rhei. „pantarhei.sk: Eseje, úvahy štúdie – Mlčanie." Accessed February 20, 2017. http://www.pantarhei.sk/knihy/beletria/eseje-uvahy-studie/mlcanie.html.

Petit press. „sme.sk: Rádio Viva má reláciu, v ktorej sa hovorí o tajomných skupinkách ovládajúcich svet." Accessed December 12, 2016. https://ekonomika.sme.sk/c/6861098/radio-viva-ma-relaciu-v-ktorej-sa-hovori-o-tajomnych-skupinkach-ovladajucich-svet.html.

Pirošík, V. „Zákon o slobodnom prístupe k informáciám: štruktúra a uplatňovanie." In *Korupcia na Slovensku a jej spracovanie v médiách*, edited by Nagyová, I. and E. Žitňanský, 59–64. Bratislava: Róbert Vico-vydavateľstvo, 2001.

PK. „*Kotleba dostal pozemky pod Krásnou Hôrkou*". Aktuality.sk (2012): online. http://www.aktuality.sk/clanok/205441/kotleba-dostal-pozemky-pod-krasnou-horkou/ (accessed January 25, 2017).

Polakevičová, I. "Controversy of media discourses in (A)political campaigns to referendum for protection of family 2015 in media space in Slovakia." In *European journal of science and theology* 12, no. 3 (2016): 11–19.

Poláš, M. „*Kočner: Lipšic donášal novinárom. Podľa Grendela je hovorcom Bašternáka.*" Medialne (2016): online. http://medialne.etrend.sk/tlac/lipsic-podla-kocnera-poskytoval-novinarom-informacie-z-vysetrovania.html (accessed February 2, 2017).

Poradca podnikateľa. „manazerskecentrum.sk: Profil autora." Accessed December 12, 2016, http://bc.aion.cz/vyhladavanie/autor/marian-benka.

Priestor i. „priestori.sk: Zem a vek nebezpečných konšpirácií." Accessed January 7, 2017, http://www.priestori.sk/zem-a-vek-nebezpecnych-konspiracii-priestori/.

Protiprúd. „protiprud.sk: Články autora Peter Sanve." Accessed January 7, 2017, http://www.protiprud.sk/autor/304.htm.

PSP ČR. „Zákon č. 348/2005 Sb. Zákon o rozhlasových a televizních poplatcích a o změně některých zákonů." Accessed January 12, 2017. https://www.zakonyprolidi.cz/cs/2005-348.

Rada Európy. Dohovor *o ochrane ľudských práv a základných slobôd. Konsolidované znenie.* Štrasburg: Rada Európy, 1950. http://www.echr.coe.int/documents/convention_slk.pdf (accessed December 27, 2016).

Rada Európy. *Európsky dohovor o cezhraničnej televízii. Konsolidovaná verzia Európskeho dohovoru o cezhraničnej televízii v znení Pozmeňujúceho protokolu.* Štrasburg: Rada Európy, 1989. http://www.rvr.sk/sk/spravy/index.php?aktualitaId=24 (accessed December 27, 2016).

Rada Európy. *Recommendation CM/Rec(2007)3 of the Committee of Ministers to member states on the remit of public service media in the information society.* Štrasburg: Rada Európy, 2007. https://wcd.coe.int/ViewDoc.jsp?id=1089759 (accessed December 27, 2016).

Rauch, J. "Exploring the alternative – mainstream dialectic: What "alternative media" means to a hybrid audience," *Communication, culture & critique* 8, no. 1 (2015): 124–143.

Redakcia. „*Téma mesiaca: Boj s rakovinou je podvod,"* Zem a vek 2, no. 11 (2014): 24–25.

Remišová, A. *Etika médií.* Bratislava: Kaligram, 2010.

Rodriguez, C. "Fissures in the mediascape: An international study of citizens media," Creskill, NJ: Hampton Press, 2001 in Rauch, J. "Exploring the alternative – mainstream dialectic: What "alternative media" means to a hybrid audience," *Communication, culture & critique* 8, no. 1 (2015): 124–143.

Rosinský, R. „Rómovia v číslach na Slovensku a v Nitrianskom kraji." In *Odlišnosti by nás mali spájať – nie rozdeľovať!,* edited by K. Vanková, 92–117. Nitra: OZ Sponka, 2014.

Rožňová, J. *Výtvarné artefakty v printovej reklame.* Nitra: Filozofická fakulta Univerzity Konštantína Filozofa v Nitre, 2014.

RTVS. „O 5 minút 12." Accessed January 15, 2017. http://www.rtvs.sk/televizia/archiv/11680/115253.

RTVS. „Štatút programových pracovníkov a spolupracovníkov RTVS." Accessed January 15, 2017. www.rtvs.org/o-rtvs/statut-rozhlasu-a-televizie-slovenska.

RTVS. „Zmluva o zabezpečení služieb verejnosti v oblasti televízneho a rozhlasového vysielania 2013-2017." Accessed January 15, 2017. http://www.rtvs.org/o-rtvs/dolezite-dokumenty-rtvs/zmluva-so-statom.

RTVS. *Výročná správa o činnosti Rozhlasu a televízie Slovenska za rok 2015.* Bratislava: RTVS, 2016. http://www.rtvs.org/o-rtvs/vyrocne-spravy/vyrocne-spravy-rtvs (accessed December 27, 2016).

RTVS. *Výročná správa o činnosti Rozhlasu a televízie Slovenska za rok 2014*. Bratislava: RTVS, 2015. http://www.rtvs.org/o-rtvs/vyrocne-spravy/vyrocne-spravy-rtvs (accessed December 27, 2016).

Schulz, W. *Politische Kommunikation. Theoretische Ansätze und Ergebnisse empirischer Forschung zur Rolle der Massenmedien in der Politik. 2. Vollstandig uberarbeitete und erweiterte Auflage.* Wiesbaden: VS Verlag für Sozialwissenschaften, 2008.

Sičáková-Beblavá, E., G. Šípoš and M. Kurian, „Korupcia a protikorupčná politika na Slovensku 1989–2010." *Forum Historiae 5*, no 2 (2011): 157–97.

SITA. „*Frešo chce búrať osady a čierne stavby.*" Sme.sk (2012): online. http://domov.sme.sk/c/6453886/freso-chce-burat-osady-a-cierne-stavby. html (accessed January 25, 2017).

Sofian, „zemavek.sk: Nikdy som sa nestretol s tým, že by Zem a vek odrádzal od návštevy lekára." Accessed December 15, 2016. http:// zemavek.sk/articles/view/mudr-lakota-nikde-som-sa-nestretol-s-tym-ze-by-zem-a-vek-odradzal-od-navstevy-lekara.

Sofian, „zemavek.sk: Vznikla asociácia nezávislých médií." Accessed December 15, 2016. http://www.zemavek.sk/articles/view/ vznikla-asociacia-nezavislych-medii.

Sofian. „mlcanie.sk: archív." Accessed February 20, 2017, http://mlcanie. sk/category/audio/page/31/.

Sofian. „zemavek.sk: Archív časopisov – august 2014." Accessed November 15, 2016, http://www.zemavek.sk/journals/view/ august-2014-2014.

Sofian. „zemavek.sk: Archív časopisov – február 2015." Accessed November 15, 2016, http://www.zemavek.sk/journals/view/ februr-2015-2015.

Sofian. „zemavek.sk: Archív časopisov – január 2016." Accessed November 15, 2016, http://www.zemavek.sk/journals/view/janur-2016.

Sofian. „zemavek.sk: Archív časopisov – máj 2013." Accessed November 15, 2016, http://www.zemavek.sk/journals/view/maj-2013.

Stereon, „Radia.sk: Počúvanosť 2+3 vlna 2012." Accessed October 30, 2016. https://www.radia.sk/pocuvanost/mml-tgi/vlny/2012-3.

Struhárik, F. „*Spisovateľ a novinár Karel Hvížďala: Naše médiá ešte nikdy neboli lepšie.*" SME (2013): online. https://ekonomika.sme.

sk/c/6759765/spisovatel-a-novinar-karel-hvizdala-nase-media-este-nikdy-neboli-lepsie.html (accessed January 31, 2017).

Šípoš, G. „Amíci si dvojičky odpálili sami, Obamova manželka je rasistka." Accessed December 12, 2016. https://spw.blog.sme.sk/c/210860/STV-Amici-si-dvojicky-odpalili-sami-Obamova-manzelka-je-rasistka.html.

Šípoš, G. *Vlastníctvo médií a jeho dosah na nezávislosť a pluralitu médií.* Bratislava: INEKO, 2004.

Školkay, A. „Strážcovia cností a žurnalistika morálneho rozhorčenia. Investigatívna žurnalistika a jej základné prvky." In *Korupcia na Slovensku a jej spracovanie v médiách*, edited by Nagyová, I. and E. Žitňanský, 81–87. Bratislava: Róbert Vico-vydavateľstvo, 2001.

Šnídl, V. „*Kto riadi proruský web Hlavné správy? Muž, ktorý neodmieta ani eurofondy.*" Dennikn.sk (2016): online. https://dennikn.sk/521950/kto-riadi-prorusky-web-hlavne-spravy-muz-ktory-neodmieta-ani-eurofondy-2/ (accessed January 25, 2017).

Štětka, V., „The watchdogs that only bark? Media and political accountability in Central and Eastern Europe," In *Journalism that matters. Views from Central and Eastern Europe*, edited by Glowacky, M., E. Lauk and A. Balcytiene, 35–60. New York: Peter Lang.

TASR and M. Kapusta. „*Európska komisia a mimovládna organizácia navrhujú zlúčiť špeciálne školy so zaostávajúcimi Rómami s bežnými školami.*" Hlavnespravy.sk (2016): online. http://www.hlavnespravy.sk/europska-komisia-a-mimovladna-organizacia-navrhuju-zlucit-specialne-skoly-so-zaostavajucimi-romami-s-beznymi-skolami/781391 (accessed January 25, 2017).

TASR. „*Kotleba považuje domy Rómov za odpad, ktorý chce zlikvidovať.*" HN.online.sk (2012): online. http://hn.hnonline.sk/slovensko-119/kotleba-povazuje-domy-romov-za-odpad-ktory-chce-zlikvidovat-503053 (accessed January 25, 2017).

Thomson, J. B. *Média a modernita.* Praha: Karolinum, 2004.

Tomalová, J., Podtatranské noviny. *There is one school in the village. Still, it is still unclear whether the second will come.* Podtatranské noviny (2017). http://www.podtatranske-noviny.sk/2017/09/starosta-rakus-nikto-mi-nevie-povedat-ako-ma-20-percentna-vacsina-integrovat-romov/ (accessed January 12, 2018)

US Census Buerau. "US Census Bureau." Accessed January 20, 2017. http://www.census.gov/popclock/.

US department of labor. "Bureau of labor statistics." Accessed January 20, 2017. https://www.bls.gov/news.release/empsit.nr0.htm

Vávra, M. „Tři přístupy k analýze diskurzu – neslučitelnost nebo možnost syntézy?" In *Miscellanea Sociologica 2006*, edited by R. Tichý, 49–65. Praha: Fakulta sociálních věd UK, 2006.

Veverková, V. *Bulvár a bulvarizácia dennej tlače.* Ljubljana: KUD Apokalipsa, 2014.

VoorhoofD. et al and T. McGonagle (eds). *Freedom of expression, the media and journalists: Case-law of the European Court of Human Rights, IRIS Themes.* Štrasburg: European Audiovisual Observatory, 2015. https://www.ivir.nl/publicaties/download/1644.pdf (accessed January 31, 2017).

Vybíral, Z. *Psychologie komunikace.* Praha: Portál, 2009.

W Press, „tyzden.sk: Planéta Rostas." Accessed November 2, 2016. https://www.tyzden.sk/casopis/15016/plan-ta-rostas/.

Waltz, M. *Alternative and activist media.* Edinburgh: Edinburgh University Press, 2005.

Weisenbacher, P. „Vtáčkovia, siroty a blázni na rádiu Viva." Accessed January 10, 2017, http://www.jetotak.sk/editorial/ vtackovia-siroty-a-blazni-na-radiu-viva.

Willett, C. "*The state of alternative publishing in America: issues and implications for libraries,*" *Counterpoise* 3, no. 1 (1999): 14.

Youtube. „Audi alteram partem 05.12.2014 Ľubomír Huďo." https:// www.youtube.com/watch?v=iBbr1lDe8Q0 (accessed December 20, 2016).

Youtube. „Havranovo talk show. hostia: Tibor Eliot Rostas a Juraj Smatana." https://www.youtube.com/watch?v=ONr6uHAD-hM (accessed December 20, 2016).

Youtube: „Relácia Mlčanie – 001. Mlčanie." https://www.youtube.com/ watch?v=qcyqZBlxGEM (accessed December 20, 2016).

Zemanovičová, D. and E. Sičáková, „Hovoriť o korupcii je málo." In *Korupcia na Slovensku a jej spracovanie v médiách*, edited by Nagyová, I. and E. Žitňanský, 8–9. Bratislava: Róbert Vico-vydavateľstvo, 2001.

Images:

Banášová, L. *Corruption and media*, private archive.

Bohuš, A. *The headquarters of Slovakia Radio in Bratislava*, private archive.

Council of Europe. *Logo of Council of Europe* (Accessible: https://www.coe.int/documents/16695/994584/COE-Logo-Quadri.png/ee7b1fc6-055b-490b-a59b-a65969e440a2?t=1371222819000, online).

Denník N Daily. *Print screen of the first website created in 2014* (Accessible on: http://www.opentat.sk/post/99715656100/pre%C4%8Do-odch%C3%A1dzame-z-denn%C3%ADka-sme). The trademark "DENNÍK N" is registered by the Slovak Industry Property Office under the No. 240702.

Dobrotková, M. *Headquarters of ESET*, private archive.

Dobrotková, M. *Headquarters of J&T and JOJ Television*, private archive.

Dobrotková, M. *Headquarters of Slovak television*, private archive.

Dobrotková, M. *The Heart of Europe, the Memorial of Velvet Revolution*, private archive.

Kollár, B. *Facebook account of Boris Kollár* (Accessible: https://www.facebook.com/boris.kollar, online).

RTVS. *Print screen from the discussion program broadcasted by RTVS on 21/01/2018* (Accessible: http://www.rtvs.sk/televizia/archiv/13004/145992, online).

Zem & Vek. *Print screen from the web site of the journal Zem & Vek* (Accessible: http://zemavek.sk/vznikla-asociacia-nezavislych-medii/, online).

About the Authors

Mgr. Artur Bekmatov, Phd.
Constantine the Philosopher
University in Nitra,
Faculty of Arts, Department of
Journalism,
B. Slančíkovej 1, 949 74 Nitra,
Slovak Republic
e-mail: artur.bekmatov@ukf.sk

Mgr. Miroslava Dobrotková, Phd.
Constantine the Philosopher
University in Nitra,
Faculty of Arts, Department of
Journalism,
B. Slančíkovej 1, 949 74 Nitra,
Slovak Republic
e-mail: mdobrotkova@ukf.sk

**Mgr. Andrea Chlebcová
Hečková, Phd.**
Constantine the Philosopher
University in Nitra,
Faculty of Arts, Department of
Journalism,
B. Slančíkovej 1, 949 74 Nitra,
Slovak Republic
e-mail: acheckova@ukf.sk

Mgr. Ján Kuciak, Phd.
† 21.2.2018
Constantine the Philosopher
University in Nitra,
Faculty of Arts, Department of
Journalism,
B. Slančíkovej 1, 949 74 Nitra,
Slovak Republic

Studies in Communication and Politics

Edited by Bogusława Dobek-Ostrowska and Michał Głowacki

www.peterlang.com